T0129673

THE BOUNCE

30 Days to a Happier You

Let your thought life create your new better life!

RONALD D. WALTERS

WESTBOW
PRESS®
A DIVISION OF THOMAS NELSON
& ZONDERVAN

Copyright © 2023 Ronald D. Walters.

All rights reserved. No part of this book may be used or reproduced by any means, graphic, electronic, or mechanical, including photocopying, recording, taping or by any information storage retrieval system without the written permission of the author except in the case of brief quotations embodied in critical articles and reviews.

WestBow Press books may be ordered through booksellers or by contacting:

WestBow Press
A Division of Thomas Nelson & Zondervan
1663 Liberty Drive
Bloomington, IN 47403
www.westbowpress.com
844-714-3454

Because of the dynamic nature of the Internet, any web addresses or links contained in this book may have changed since publication and may no longer be valid. The views expressed in this work are solely those of the author and do not necessarily reflect the views of the publisher, and the publisher hereby disclaims any responsibility for them.

Any people depicted in stock imagery provided by Getty Images are models, and such images are being used for illustrative purposes only. Certain stock imagery © Getty Images.

Scripture quotations marked KJV are from the Holy Bible, King James Version (Authorized Version). First published in 1611. Quoted from the KJV Classic Reference Bible, Copyright © 1983 by The Zondervan Corporation.

Scripture quotations marked NASB are taken from the New American Standard Bible®, Copyright © 1960, 1962, 1963, 1968, 1971, 1972, 1973, 1975, 1977, 1995 by The Lockman Foundation. Used by permission.

ISBN: 978-1-6642-9301-4 (sc)
ISBN: 978-1-6642-9299-4 (hc)
ISBN: 978-1-6642-9300-7 (e)

Library of Congress Control Number: 2023903470

Print information available on the last page.

WestBow Press rev. date: 8/22/2023

I dedicate this book to my wife and lifetime partner, Suzanne, the ten beautiful children we share, and all of those who came along through marriage and birth and made our lives a beautiful bounce back.

CONTENTS

PART V: WORDS

PART I

....

EMPATHY

DEVELOPING THE ABILITY TO FEEL ALLOWS RELATIONSHIPS TO BE REAL

Prethought: Using tough times to develop a soft heart

"Whatever Your Mind Can Conceive
and Believe, It Can Achieve." –
– NAPOLEON HILL

"We become what we think about most of the
time, and that's the strangest secret."
– EARL NIGHTINGALE

As you consider the steps outlined in this book to becoming a happier you, I want to give you a bit of background about me. I was the youngest in a family of six siblings, raised in a small town in Wisconsin. I've experienced various trauma in more than one area during my lifetime. For instance, during my early childhood years, I was victimized and brutalized by bullies and other predators, including peers and disgruntled classmates, throughout elementary and junior high school. This trauma continued into my adult years, and each time I was devastated. As I climbed the corporate ladder by succeeding in business and sales, I was disappointed by territorial conflicts, lost opportunities resulting from nepotism, and general mistreatment by those who should have otherwise contributed to my success.

Two things that affected my early life, with which I credit any success in my present life: (1) my experience with Jesus Christ at a young age and (2) my personal development through the ministry of God's work! As a young man, I was enthralled with advanced-level basketball players and their incredible energy and focused prethought. Their ball handling, court intuition, tenacity, and focus left me mesmerized anytime I watched these talented athletes compete. I was fascinated by their intuitive nature as they moved around the court and their lightning-quick decisions, whether passing, defending, or shooting. I learned that they were so advanced in these skills because of personal discipline and practice, practice, practice. Their minds and bodies worked in complete harmony because they had, for years, prepared for shooting, running, and all other aspects of the game. By the time such players competed in a game, they had thousands of hours of dedicated pre-game drills under their belt. Their movements in the game become natural to what they had prepared for through practice and drills. Their hard work created patterns.

As an example of prethought lifestyle, consider building a happy marriage. Focusing on monogamous marriage and meditating on the oneness you can achieve with your spouse--this is a positive marital 'prethought!' With this paradigm, your marriage will heat up. You'll not waste energy on affairs, fighting, or distancing techniques! The prethought of making your marriage great will destroy the paradigm of letting your marriage disintegrate.

As I mentioned, I endured some difficult times as a human being. Yet, my life is strangely and wonderfully peaceful and joyous. I credit that outcome to the constant pursuit of prepared thinking or prethought! Instinctive decision-making is easier than deliberating over life's complex execution. I have navigated complex issues like a point guard driving to the hoop for an easy lay-up—all due to having the proper mindset.

The ultimate positive change in my life came when my now ex-wife ended a tumultuous marriage by telling me that she planned to divorce me. At the time, I was enjoying ministerial success with a fast-growing church, business success in the life insurance industry, and meaningful relationships with successful ministers who offered me mentorship and friendship. I didn't realize it then, but my divorce was a turning point. It also became an altar upon which I could thank God for this process and, most importantly, for the people I would later meet. I faced financial distress, an anti-male divorce court, and only being allowed to "visit" with my children. I also grappled with an imploding ministerial future because of my marital problems and the opinions of my professional colleagues. Simultaneously, I worried about how this would affect my children and the children of the woman I would choose to partner with in marriage going forward.

I grew from being a latchkey, abandoned child in my early life into a strong, determined, and energetic self-thinker. Still, I had found myself in the throes of a divorce, a debilitating back injury, a subsequent surgery, income loss, and a damaged reputation. I have felt judged by friends and family about my role in the brokenness my life had become. I am building a successful ministry and growing a family with six biological children and four stepchildren. I could have ventured into a life of despair from where I was, using every opportunity to become even more embittered, but I chose to become better instead.

This first day of becoming a happier you is celebrating what we call "empathy." Within the pages of this writing are ideas and suggestions from someone who had entered terrible brokenness that culminated with the separation and the divorce of my first marriage decades ago. Most of what you'll read reflects the principles I have utilized to create a much happier version of myself. I spend more time with myself than anybody else! In your pursuit of empathy, recognize that other people have experienced hardship, trauma, and disillusionment like yours. People have not picked us up but have let us down. I trust you'll enjoy the rest of these writings and reflections from my heart to yours. What follows are my thoughts from my morning devotions and the pursuit of trying to be a happier me. Please make this a part of your morning devotions as you work to discover a happier YOU!

Ronald D. Walters

NOTES

PART II

EMOTIONS

THE BOUNCE

THE CONTAGIOUS POWER OF EMOTION

Prethought: Stabilized emotion equals less commotion. No one regrets what they don't say!

You can tell a lot about how a person feels based on facial expressions, gestures, intonation, and cadence of speech. This focus on the emotional states of others is good, but we also need to pay attention to our own emotions. We often "catch" feelings from those around us. Nicholas Christakis and James Fowler's research shows that happiness can be spread as quickly as a virus. This process is known as "emotional contagion." In 2008, Christakis and Fowler published the results of a study in which they followed 4,739 people for twenty years and intermittently surveyed their happiness. An individual's happiness is a ripple effect that flows through social groups to affect those not even connected to the original individual. Additionally, for every happy person in a group, the joy of everyone in the group goes up by 9 percent.[1]

Christakis and Fowler's research shows that those around us influence our happiness. However, emotional contagion also occurs with negative emotions, which can be detrimental to our emotion-based close relationships. The anger, stress, or sadness of someone close to us can profoundly affect our moods. Our emotions can influence others just as strongly as if they experienced it themselves. Our brains deal with second-hand emotions as if they were our own. Negative emotions can lead to deeper health issues such as heart disease. Second-hand stress can also create rifts in our relationships with our loved ones. Unfortunately, it's easier to "catch" negative emotions than positive ones, and people who are more sensitive to the feelings of others are more susceptible to emotional contagion.[2] Negative emotions like stress and anger destroy our brains' judgment and memory portions. Continuous anger can severely affect personal relationships and even job performance.[3]

The Pastor's Perspective

Sometimes, individuals believe they have a "right" to be pessimistic. They let their negative emotions and thought processes run wild. The article above concludes that unhappiness breeds unhappiness, depression breeds depression, and anger breeds anger! You may feel a right to spray your negativity and spread your emotional contagion to the people around you, but recognize how unhealthy your virus of negativity affects those around you.

You might stay at home, coughing and sneezing from inside your little world of hurt, and still expose your spouse, children, acquaintances, and business partners to a virus that can bring even significant corporations to their knees. Think of that adverse effect going into your children's ears or the heart of your spouse, whom you agreed to love, honor, and cherish. According to the research, I can directly cause stress to my children, marriage, and social groups if I decide to be angry. If I choose to be depressed, I can easily set in motion the depression of my entire family. It is selfish and ignorant to allow myself to impose negative consequences on my children and vicariously on my grandchildren.

Ronald D. Walters

"Be careful for nothing, but in everything by prayer and supplication with thanksgiving let your requests be made known unto God. And the peace of God, which passeth all understanding, shall keep your hearts and minds through Christ Jesus. Finally, brethren, whatsoever things are true, honest, pure, lovely, and of good report; if there be any virtue and praise, think on these things. Those things, which ye have both learned, and received, and heard, and seen in me, do and the God of peace shall be with you." (Philippians 4:6-9 KJV)

I can choose to give the gift of God's peace to my spouse, my children, and heirs that follow for many generations. Because of my controlled emotions, they will receive a gift allowing them to live in happiness and contentment throughout the ages. Through Christ, I can accomplish this gift.

Meditate on and believe in the Word of God that your life is good with proper prethought. Your life shall become that gift, and you shall become a positive emotional contagion to the little ones. Come on, Christian, start right now! Stop the negativity and start releasing God through your thoughts to provide yourself with an expected positive life. Those close to you will thank you.

NOTES

Ronald D. Walters

DAY 3: EMOTION LESSON 2

ANXIETY

Prethought: Anxiety is not my friend.
Through self-control I'll make it end!

To understand anxiety, we first need to understand cognition. Cognition refers to the mental action or process of acquiring knowledge and understanding through thought, experience, and the senses. Cognition is how we understand the world around us and interpret how the world affects us.[4] When our brains incorrectly interprets the world, our bodies respond with panic. If this occurs regularly and consistently, especially if it interferes with the ability to perform our daily routines, it can be diagnosed as a panic disorder. Panic disorder strikes without reason or warning, causing sudden fear, anxiety attacks, and physical symptoms such as a racing heart.[5]

Most people feel small amounts of anxiety in regular life, and this can even be beneficial. Anxiety disorders, however, cause such a high level of stress that individuals can no longer lead normal lives. Anxiety disorders involve not only feelings of fear but also physiological effects like an increased heart rate, sweating, or blurry vision. An anxiety disorder can be diagnosed if the response is inappropriate for the situation, cannot be controlled, or interferes with normal functioning.

Types of anxiety disorders include the following:

- ✓ Panic Disorder, where intense feelings of terror occur suddenly and, often, without reason.
- ✓ Post-traumatic stress disorder (PTSD), which develops after an intensely stressful event.
- ✓ Social anxiety disorder, or a fear of social interactions.
- ✓ Specific phobias or fears about a particular object or situation.
- ✓ Generalized anxiety disorder, which is intense, unprovoked worry.

Anxiety disorders are the most common form of diagnosable mental illness and affect more women than men. The precise cause is still unknown, but chemical imbalances most likely cause anxiety disorders in the brain.[6]

The Pastor's Perspective

 Science helps to explain why the God who created you offered a "word" that speaks directly to managing what has become a regular part of the human experience, the emotion of anxiety! A guiding principle I have used in my life is, "I cannot control what happens to me. I can only control what happens in me." I have developed a steadfast and unmovable opinion because I must keep my emotions free of clutter, which typically remains in the human mind. I've tried to love God, prioritize relationships around me, love people, and then go about doing business so I can provide for others. Where is the harm in that? However, I have noticed people will do and say all manner of evil against me. I also experienced physical abuse in my childhood and emotional abuse in my adulthood. Still, I'm just trying to be me at the end of the day! Therefore, I have learned the same lesson as every other human

Ronald D. Walters

through experience. I have gone through a divorce and needed to speak to a therapist. I have experienced and still experience pain, suffering, and anxiety.

Early in my adulthood, I became a Christian and began to trust something other than people, but I still had to live with people and have good relationships with them. However, I am not required to trust that what people say is or will be valid. Instead, I know they speak words and show actions to me from their perception of how the world is to them. For example, if I encounter a judgmental person who may not like something about me, I am not required to perceive myself the way they do. Positive prethought about myself becomes a defense against the temptation to perceive myself through the eyes of another person's judgment.

Christians have a significant advantage, as we can see ourselves through the Word of God. Our loving Father says through love that, without Christ, I am a sinner and, as a sinner, need repentance. When exposed to this truth rather than self-justification, I sought the Word to discover why God would think I needed repentance. By seeking the Word, I needed to repent for the things my sin had left inside me. I also had to repent for what others tried to attach to me through their actions, facial expressions, angry words, and distractions created by their judgmental nature.

Through studying the Word, I now understand that unpleasant experiences with angry and judgmental people showed me how they spoke from their personal experiences and how they saw me. Those negative experiences could have devastated my self-worth without a proper self-sense of who I am through Christ. By knowing Him and His Word, I now see myself through His paradigm and live in the "newness of life." With this paradigm as my prethought, I am far less prone to anxiety, panic attacks, and terrible thoughts and accusations toward those close to me. I can live in "God's peace and joy." As a pastor, I hope you have this same kind of worry-free living through a self-image built through a prethought life based on the Word of the Lord. A Christ-centered prethought will empower you to choose whether you accept the opinions of others in the world as a definition of who you are or if you take the opinion of God and grow to be who He has called you to be.

At this time, meditate on the verses mentioned listed below. Take note of Ecclesiastes 11:10, where the central message is to forgive childhood. Recognizing the Word of God calls us to forgive what happened to us in early life. Impress into your heart the cross of Christ. Notice where He said, "Father, forgive them, for they do not know what they do." On Easter Sunday, where we all think about the great sacrifice Jesus made on the cross. Only a few of us celebrate His three days in the tomb. This time of year gives me hope because He was resurrected from the dead. It is possible to emerge from the tomb of childhood fear or adult anxiety. Then, you can begin to put into people the things you glean from God's Word. It is time you rise and walk in the way Christ called you!

If you allow anxiety, missed thoughts, and panic attacks to define the existence you choose on earth, you will affect those around you like a virus. Let's put anxiety under the blood of Jesus! Forgive the people around us and what we have allowed to happen inside us, and rise and walk through the work of the cross into this world with joy and peace. Come on, Christian, love the people around you, don't judge them, and don't hurt them with your thoughts and actions. Right now, choose to create an atmosphere of love, peace, and joy. Then, you're going to become the solution instead of adding to the continual problematic issues of the human experience! Remember, Paul said, "Forgetting those things behind, I press toward the mark of the high calling in Christ!" You are to be resurrected from the tomb into a new life with God free from the death of sin.

Truckers used to say, "Hey, good buddy, got your ears on?" I say, "Do you have ears to hear what the Spirit is saying to you?"

KEY VERSES

- "He also that received seed among the thorns is he that heareth the word; and the care of this world, and the deceitfulness of riches, choke the word, and he becometh unfruitful." (Matthew 13:22 KJV)

Ronald D. Walters

- "Therefore remove sorrow from thy heart, and put away evil from thy flesh: for childhood and youth are vanity." (Ecclesiastes 11:10 KJV).
- "Take no thought for your life, what ye shall eat; neither for the body, what ye shall put on. The life is more than meat, and the body is more than raiment." (Luke 12:22-23 KJV)
- "Fear thou not; for I am with thee be not dismayed; for I am thy God: I will strengthen thee; yea, I will help thee; yea, I will uphold thee with the right hand of my righteousness." (Isaiah 41:10 KJV)
- "Be anxious for nothing, but in everything by prayer and supplication, with thanksgiving, let your requests be made known to God." (Philippians 4:6 NASB)

NOTES

Ronald D. Walters

THE BOUNCE

TRUST

Prethought: To feel close, I will trust and
the shackles of fear I will bust!

When it comes to trusting others, people generally either trust others or they don't. Those who distrust tend to assume the worst in others and keep them at a distance, so they won't be disappointed. Conversely, those who over-trust tend to believe the best in others and are shocked when someone breaks that trust. We need to find a balance between the two extremes. Trust should be gained not only by words but by actions. Here are four key principles to remember when deciding to trust a new person. First, trustworthy people will have open and honest communication about their feelings. Hiding feelings leads to resentment in any relationship. Second, trustworthy people will create physical, emotional, or virtual boundaries. The violation of boundaries causes disrespect in the relationship. Third, trustworthy people are dependable in their promises. Breaking promises causes disappointment in the relationship. Finally, trustworthy people are predictable in their actions. Unpredictable behaviors cause doubt in the relationship. Learning to trust others is primarily about listening to your intuition and knowledge.[7]

The Pastor's Perspective

A particular biblical concept that is important for human beings to understand before entering into any human relationship is trust.

Romans 3:3-4 says: "For what if some did not believe. Shall their unbelief make the faith of God without effect? God forbid yea, let God be true, but every man a liar; as it is written, that thou mightest be justified in thy sayings, and mightest overcome when thou art judged." (KJV)

Consider what David wrote in Psalms. He was just a king of many, many people. What did he know? David knew he could choose to either trust or mistrust God. How David overcame his personal life as a King would have been impossible if he did not understand an essential truth. All humans have failure built into them, but we can trust God. The foundation of this truth makes it okay for me to get to know people, accept those people as they are, and enjoy a continuous relationship with those people while I am living on this earth. Let's take a look at a few Psalms.

- "And the LORD shall help them, and deliver them: he shall deliver them from the wicked, and save them because they trust in him." (Psalms 37:40 KJV)

David gives us a fundamental principle: God is trustworthy and should be the one we trust. God is our defender, redeemer, and deliverer. People will let us down, but the Lord will always sustain us. If our trust is in God and we spend our earthly time getting to know Him through study, devotions, prayer, and personal and community worship, we feel 'safe.' He is the priority relationship since we find comfort, direction, instruction, and righteousness within the context of our trust in the Lord. He will make all things right if those around us mistreat us. We don't have to judge the people around us because He is their judge. We only have to love the people around us because He is our judge. When we place trust in God, we can love people no matter what their behaviors try to make us think about them. If our trust is only in people who say they love God, we might blame God when they disappoint us. However,

Ronald D. Walters

if our trust is accurately placed solely in the Lord, people's actions are less influential in developing our trust. Trust allows us to have peace and enjoy every day to the fullest.

I've learned that all people are a disappointment at one time or another. My Lord has never once been a disappointment with all my heart. I'd rather trust that God is true and recognize that every person who walks the earth has the potential to lie, mistreat, abandon, and even not genuinely love me. That is the human experience, where these things happen to every person and every relationship. To myself, I have had to say, "Get over it!" The Word of God says all people are going to fail. It also tells us that, in all situations, God never fails. Trust in the Lord is the foundation of all prethought. I can expect to be disappointed by those around me. Yet, I expect never to be disappointed by the God within me. He has asked me to trust Him. He can also ask me to "love [my] enemies" because my trust in Him will compensate me for the pain and sorrow I received from those enemies. My trust is in God. Therefore, He can ask me to "take up my cross and follow Him" because nothing reflects the brokenness man gives to others more than what we did to Him on the cross. I can trust this God who walked among us with love the whole time, knowing we would crucify Him with hate.

I trust in God because I know that, to enjoy my human experience, I must love those around me who, according to the Word, are "liars"! Jesus said of himself, "I am the Way, the truth, the life." Come on, Christian! Put your trust in God and release everyone else to be human so you can fill your brief time on earth with love, joy, peace, gentleness, meekness, self-control, goodness, and faith!

Key Verses

- "Shiggaion of David, which he sang unto the LORD, concerning the words of Cush the Benjamite. O LORD my God, in thee do I put my trust: save me from all of them that persecute me, and deliver me." (Psalms 7:1 KJV)

- "And they that know thy name will put their trust in thee: for thou, LORD, hast not forsaken them that seek thee." (Psalms 9:10 KJV)
- "Trust in the LORD, and do good; [so] shalt thou dwell in the land, and verily thou shalt be fed." (Psalms 37:3 KJV)
- "Commit thy way unto the LORD; trust also in him; and he shall bring [it] to pass." (Psalms 37:5 KJV)

Ronald D. Walters

NOTES

THE BOUNCE

SADNESS

Prethought: I will embrace sadness for a time but realize happiness is the real friend of mine.

From an early age, we learn to avoid sad feelings. Crying children are silenced and told, "It's okay, you're fine," which teaches them that being sad is bad or wrong. Children don't have the vocabulary to describe their feelings. Still, they will remember the emotions, and the feelings will affect them for the rest of their lives. The caregiver's job is to help children develop ways to express and deal with their emotions. Sadness differs from depression because sadness is a natural response to life events and experiences. Depression, on the other hand, often happens without warning or explanation. Depression suppresses other emotions so that we feel no emotions. Sadness, however, helps us see what we value most in life. According to psychologist Robert Firestone, "When we feel sadness, it centers us"[8]. Depression often makes us scared that feeling sad will release all of the emotions that have been suppressed. The feeling-suppressing methods we develop as children often affect our adult lives. Psychologist Lisa Firestone says, "We can't selectively numb pain without numbing joy"[9] Suppressing sadness makes us less likely to be genuinely happy.

Ronald D. Walters

The Pastor's Perspective

"But when the young man heard that saying, he went away sorrowful: for he had great possessions." (Matthew 19:22 KJV)

Consider the first example of sorrow in the rich young ruler who "had great possessions." For this discussion, this could be either material things or, for most of us who lack material wealth, it can reflect emotional baggage. The word "possessions" in Matthew 19 refers to "the estates" or things passed down. In perfect families, they are positive personality traits, attributes, and habits in a young person. However, in an abusive or dysfunctional family, baggage can bring sorrow. A significant quantity of depressive and sorrowful inventory is the memory of hurt, disappointments, abuse, neglect, and other painful human experiences.

"And they were exceeding sorrowful, and began every one of them to say unto him, Lord, is it I?" (Matthew 26:22 KJV)

Those in Matthew 26 were sorrowful because they had the revelation that one would betray the Lord. In our lifetime, when we have forsaken righteousness or willingly entered into sinful behaviors, we knowingly allow ourselves to betray Christ inside us.

Jesus was right there in the room with the disciples. They were in the "presence" of the mighty God in Christ, yet still felt sorrow at the revelation of their potential to betray the person they loved. Think of someone who has betrayed you and brought your heart to a place of despair—this could be a parent, romantic partner, teacher, coach, or peer. Whatever caused you to betray Jesus, repentance should ease your sorrowful heart.

KEY VERSES

- "And he took with him Peter and the two sons of Zebedee and began to be sorrowful and very heavy. Then saith he unto them, my soul is exceeding sorrowful, even unto death: tarry ye here, and watch with me." (Matthew 26:37 KJV)

- "For his anger endureth but a moment; in his favor is life: weeping may endure for a night, but joy cometh in the morning." (Psalms 30:5 KJV)

 The Matthew 26 example of sorrow reflects the words of Jesus Christ when he felt the weight of the decision to go to the cross. It's impossible to understand what He felt because we are not the Savior. When He was the closest to fulfilling the divine call upon His life, there was a weight upon His heart that He described as "sorrowful unto death." What a sublime godly moment when we allow ourselves to become Christian. Some think this entrance into a new life is filled with joy and happiness. Yet, Isaiah describes the Savior as "a man of sorrow and acquainted with grief." Why would we want to have a life outside of what He felt?

Balance in life comes when we can steward sorrow and joy, sometimes on the same day. This good/bad, high/low scenario provides us with an opportunity to be human and Christian. To be without sorrow and the feeling of despair, we can never truly understand "the joy of the Lord is my strength." If we have sorrow and emotional pain in life, the experience of those emotions provides us with celebration when we are free from them and rise above those circumstances.

To meditate on the reality that life is challenging is a healthy thing to do. However, I don't stay there or let it be the foundation of my life. According to those three scriptures above, taking inventory of all the hurts and blessings can become a "great estate." Therefore, I need to let go and give the testimony of victory to the poor. The thought that I have betrayed the Lord brings sorrow into my life, provoking me to celebrate when I haven't broken His heart! Going to the cross to follow Him can be tough to navigate, but come on, Christian! Lay down the usual reactions to the sorrow of life, take up your cross, and follow Him into the joy of building His church! He is with you, loves you, and knows about sorrow, but He gives us "victory"!

Ronald D. Walters

NOTES

THE BOUNCE

HAPPINESS

Prethought: No matter what is happening to me, I am going to maintain the happiness within me.

The science of happiness is the study of what makes people happy. Positive psychology branches off from the study of happiness to a specific type of psychology and therapy that emphasizes the development of positive emotions. Happiness is one of the most widely researched and discussed feelings. Many studies show how our thoughts and actions affect our joy and outline the habits of genuinely happy people. For example, happy people regularly exercise and eat healthy foods, which comes from an understanding that eating healthy foods and exercising can significantly improve one's mood. Therefore, happy people tend to be physically and emotionally well. Happy people have open and honest relationships with those around them. They participate in "active-constructive responding" or express genuine interest in others' emotions and feelings and respond encouragingly. Happy people also perform acts of kindness for both strangers and acquaintances. They cultivate an atmosphere of kindness around them. Happy people have a "flow." They have motivation for what they are doing because they enjoy it. Happy people find deep meaning in their life and practice a connection to religion or spirituality to give their life a deeper meaning. Happy people use their strengths and live by their virtues. They use traits and aspects unique to them to achieve their goals. Happy people have high regard for gratitude and hope. They know that being grateful leads to other positive emotions.[10]

The Pastor's Perspective

To be happy, grow honest relationships through acts of kindness, be physically well, flow with spiritual meaning while working on your strengths, and show gratitude.

In our study, seven categories outline the habits of happy people. These practices should help us to "rejoice in the Lord always" and were established for Christians, especially those involved in a church community. They will not only verify but strengthen these patterns in daily life. Consider number one: having honest relationships and close friendships. It is better to develop close friendships with those who genuinely acknowledge that Jesus is the Lord, have repented of a lifestyle of sin, and are doing their best to live patterns of holiness.

Regarding acts of kindness, Galatians 6:10 says,

- "Do good unto all men, especially unto them who are of the household of faith."
- The ideas of exercise and finding a flow into the more profound meaning and spiritual activity sum up the notion of, "Clap your hands, all you people, and shout unto God with the voice of triumph come before his presence with singing and praise him with the dance and timbrel" (Psalm 47:1).
- Regarding gratitude, "Come before his presence with thanksgiving and into his courts with praise!" (Psalm 100).

We are taught to revere and honor leadership by communicating well with them. It is strange to me when people don't see the value of a church community and don't fight for unity in the bond of love.

I once heard a story about a stepfather who owned a ranch out west but wanted to mine for gold in California. He hastily sold his ranch to move to the West Coast, where he began to excavate a small, little claim. Sometime within the first year, he recognized that the land he had purchased in California, with the fee from the land he sold, would yield him little gold. However, the ranch he sold had a great harvest of petroleum underneath the soil. The person who bought the property the stepfather ran away from could cash in, while the stepfather sought gold and riches elsewhere. The stepfather felt the pain of a deal gone awry.

 Some Christians are like the man who sold his petroleum-rich farm for worthless land elsewhere. We become lonely, sad, and even angry at people that are living within the context of Christianity throughout a vibrant church community by isolating and pulling back from biblical mandates and patterns of involvement with others and friendships. Self-imposed exile only fosters anti-happy practices. Put down your pout, overcome your fear, enter into fellowship with the body of Christ, and you will find the seven habits of happy people. David, in Psalms, says, "Blessed is the man that walketh not in the counsel of the ungodly, nor standeth in the way of sinners, nor sitteth in the seat of the scornful. But his delight is in the law of the Lord, and in his law doth he meditate day and night."

Come on, Christian, let your love show and prosper as you prospect the gold where you are planted.

PRETHOUGHT

Happy is how I choose to be, not the place where I have decided to live.

NOTES

THE BOUNCE

DISGUST

Prethought: I will define my life through the things that please me and not meditate on those that disgust me!

Children learn the emotional response of disgust. Babies have an automatic response to distasteful food. However, there is no emotion behind this response; it is simply a sensory reaction. Studies have shown that babies will try to eat fake dog poop made out of peanut butter and cheese. Children typically begin to show disgust around age six. This propensity for aversion increases throughout adolescence and decreases into adulthood. We usually learn disgust from those around us. However, there is evidence that we are intrinsically disgusted by insects and bugs.[11]

Disgust is essential because it can tell us how the environment affects us. Disgust keeps us from getting sick by preventing us from eating rotten or poisonous foods. Similarly, disgust keeps us away from toxic people who have betrayed our trust or abused us. Validating others' disgust can decrease the anxiety and shame they feel. Disgust can be an outward physical or an internal emotional sensation. Processing disgust will help our brains return to a neutral state.[12]

Ronald D. Walters

If you were given a choice between three glasses of water—one with a bitter taste, one with arsenic, and one that had had dog poop in it but had been filtered—which would you drink? Psychology professor Paul Rozin performed a trial with a similar setup to this question. According to Rozin, disgust is based on the "knowledge of the nature of something," not necessarily the fear of sickness. Rozin found that people were less disgusted with the arsenic glass than the filtered water glass. There is a stark difference between fear and disgust. Fear is the reaction to harmful effects on our physical selves, while disgust is the reaction to the adverse effects on our souls. Researchers agree on three criteria that will make something a "core disgust."

To be a "core disgust," the object must be "something you could eat, something that has or had a life of its own, and something that has the power to make other things disgusting." This final criterion is the most central. If you didn't like carrots but were given a bowl of mashed potatoes that a carrot had fallen into and was taken out of, you would still likely eat it. However, if a bug had fallen in and were taken out, you would consider the bowl "contaminated." The phrase, "Once in contact, always in contact," similarly applies to situations with food or objects. Still, it can also apply to people who commit immoral acts. These are called sociomoral disgusts. One such example is cannibalistic serial killers in Western culture. Most serial killers are seen as despicable, but they become disgusting once they decide to eat their victims. Sociomoral disgust also varies around the world. For example, compared to people in the West, people in India are less disgusted by core disgust but much more disgusted by sociomoral disgust.[13]

The Pastor's Perspective

Scorning, according to science, is likened to disgust. In the Word of God, it indicates that when a person begins to scorn, there are four dynamics.

1. The preached word and the judgment of godly instruction cause an emotional knee-jerk reaction. The scornful person then develops a "hatred" for the preacher, not just the preached word. A scornful person causes disunity, which is common among those who hate the kingdom of heaven. A scornful person lives in contention and shares contention whenever they can.

2. A scornful person withdraws from those who have proven wisdom and understanding. They find their delight in the pathology of hate and distrust rather than delighting in the law of the Lord, as a scornful person spends little time studying the Word of God.

3. The scorner fights the works of God in a community by calling for civic authorities or the government to intimidate what they consider the work of the 'feeble' people of God.

As you look through the scripture, you'll notice sinners can repent, and the ungodly can change their ways, but scorners never seem to rise from a place called "the seat of the scornful" (Psalm 1:1 KJV). Scorning becomes a pathology that allows scorners to think of themselves above the preached Word and live outside the parameters of biblical discipline. Scorners may say they appreciate the leaders, but they withdraw and want to spend less time in the presence of the Lord. When the preaching of the Word comes across the pulpit, scorners have disgust for it and the person delivering it.

One of my simple joys is that I'm beyond concerned with people's opinions. I recognize I'm moving toward an appointment with death and, after that, the judgment. Therefore, I need to preach the Word as given, not as it would be well received. Since in the heart of man, there's extraordinarily little we find in common with the Word of God. The Word of God is constantly moving His people to higher places and locations of the greater revelation of self! The Word is about a psychological phenomenon known as disgust, which provokes secularists to the power of scorning.

Please take a minute to measure what's in your heart. How do you respond to the preaching of God's Word? That reaction will be the same as how you will react in the presence of Jesus Christ Himself at the white throne of judgment. If you find being around other Christians on this side of death difficult, what makes you think He would let you live with Christians on the other side of eternity? Rejecting His decisions for our eternal placement is like sitting in the church and scorning those trying to live for God. Those who are preaching the Word of God and those who are trying to love you through Jesus.

Come on, Christian! Don't sit, shake your head, or laugh under your breath at our efforts in the name of Jesus. Why do such things? Repent and enjoy the body of Christ. Let's all move toward victory together!

In the study of emotions, it is exciting to me how science has related disgust to a level of scorn. The Bible has a lot to say about scorners and scorning. Please read each of the following biblical examples of this lesson:

KEY VERSES

- "But when Sanballat the Horonite, and Tobiah the servant, the Ammonite, and Geshem the Arabian, heard it, they laughed us to scorn, despised us, and said, what is this thing that ye do? will ye rebel against the king?" (Nehemiah 2:19 KJV)
- "And he thought scorn to lay hands on Mordecai alone; for they had showed him the people of Mordecai: wherefore Haman sought to destroy all the Jews throughout the whole kingdom of Ahasuerus, even the people of Mordecai." (Esther 3:6 KJV)
- "I am as one mocked of his neighbor, who calleth upon God, and he answereth him: the just upright man is laughed to scorn." (Job 12:4 KJV)
- "My friends scorn me: but mine eye poureth out tears unto God." (Job 16:20 KJV)

- "The righteous see it, and are glad: and the innocent laugh them to scorn." (Job 22:19 KJV)
- "What man is like Job, who drinketh up scorning like water?" (Job 34:7 KJV)
- "He scorneth the multitude of the city, neither regardeth he the crying of the driver." (Job 39:7 KJV)

  - "We have become a reproach to our neighbors, a scorn and derision to them that are round about us." (Psalms 79:4 KJV)
  - "Blessed is the man that walketh not in the counsel of the ungodly, nor standeth in the way of sinners, nor sitteth in the seat of the scornful." (Psalms 1:1 KJV)
- "But thou art holy, O thou that inhabitest the praises of Israel. Our fathers trusted in thee: they trusted, and thou didst deliver them. They cried unto thee and were delivered: they trusted in thee and were not confounded. But I am a worm and no man; a reproach of men and despised of the people. All they that see me laugh me to scorn: they shoot out the lip, shake the head, saying, He trusted on the Lord that he would deliver him: let him deliver him, seeing he delighted in him." (Psalms 22:3-8 - KJV)
- "Thou makest us a reproach to our neighbors, a scorn and a derision to them that are round about us." (Psalms 44:13 KJV)
- "Our soul is exceedingly filled with the scorning of those that are at ease, and with the contempt of the proud." (Psalms 123:4 KJV)
- "How long, ye simple ones, will ye love simplicity? and the scorners delight in their scorning, and fools hate knowledge?" (Proverbs 1:22 KJV)
- "Surely he scorneth the scorners: but he giveth grace unto the lowly." (Proverbs 3:34 KJV)
- "He that reproveth a scorner getteth to himself shame: and he that rebuketh a wicked man getteth himself a blot." (Proverbs 9:7 KJV)
- "Reprove not a scorner, lest he hate thee: rebuke a wise man, and he will love thee." (Proverbs 9:8 KJV)

Ronald D. Walters

- "If thou be wise, thou shalt be wise for thyself: but if thou scornest, thou alone shalt bear it." (Proverbs 9:12 KJV)
- "A wise son heareth his father's instruction: but a scorner heareth not rebuke." (Proverbs 13:1 KJV)
- "A scorner seeketh wisdom, and findeth it not: but knowledge is easy unto him that understandeth." (Proverbs 14:6 KJV)
- "A scorner loveth not one that reproveth him: neither will he go unto the wise." (Proverbs 15:12 KJV)
- "Smite a scorner, and the simple will beware and reprove one that hath understanding, and he will understand knowledge." (Proverbs 19:25 KJV)
- "An ungodly witness scorneth judgment: and the mouth of the wicked devoureth iniquity." (Proverbs 19:28 KJV)
- "Judgments are prepared for scorners, and stripes for the back of fools." (Proverbs 19:29 KJV)
- "When the scorner is punished, the simple is made wise: and when the wise is instructed, he receiveth knowledge." (Proverbs 21:11 KJV)
- "Proud and haughty scorner is his name, who dealeth in proud wrath." (Proverbs 21:24 KJV)
- "Cast out the scorner, and contention shall go out; yea, strife and reproach shall cease." (Proverbs 22:10 KJV)
- "The thought of foolishness is sin: and the scorner is an abomination to men." (Proverbs 24:9 KJV)

NOTES

Ronald D. Walters

THE BOUNCE

SURPRISE

**Prethought: Celebrating surprise provokes
a positive rise in my feelings!**

Researchers have only recently begun to understand the science behind why surprise pleases us. When we are given surprise gifts, our brains' pleasure center receives dopamine, which floods our bodies with a comfortable feeling. That shot of dopamine makes our brain want more of whatever elicited it in the first place, making us want more surprises. Dopamine increases attraction and excitement, which then improves our relationships. Since surprise shows us something we do not know, it can help our brain make new neural pathways with further information. Our brains are designed to enjoy new stimuli. When we experience something new, our brain releases pleasure-inducing dopamine.

Additionally, surprise heightens our happiness from good surprises, making the sadness felt by negative surprises even more devastating. Surprise helps the brain focus on new stimuli, due to the brain releasing a shot of noradrenaline, which activates the fight-or-flight response.

The repeated dopamine release during surprises has also been measured to reduce anxiety and depression. The most beneficial type of surprise is awe which we feel when we see something impressive or powerful. Being in awe has been measured to decrease inflammatory chemicals in our bodies.[14]

The Pastor's Perspective

When did walking with God become boring? Think precisely about when you lost your excitement about His presence and people and, more importantly, when you lost the <u>awe</u> at His Word.

In the puniness of our thinking, we consider fearing the Lord as being in a position where we should run and hide from God because 'He's going to get us.' We feel that because we are on the wrong side of the relationship. We think He will get us because we do not understand His nature, nor do we desire to be excited about or surprised by Him or His actions.

 A relationship that has lost the 'awe' can be described as dull or lacking stimulation. Thus, the relationship has become less valuable and much less rewarding to those in that boring relationship. We know that the Word became flesh and dwelt among us. We understand that we are to have a relationship with the Word as it manifests as a physical person. Then, it would stand to reason that our relationship with God has the potential to become dull, unstimulating, and, therefore, not fulfilling at all. The opposite is true; it can be stimulating, exciting, and fulfilling. The choice is up to you.

Suppose we have a relationship with a member of the opposite sex, and they send us a note telling us they find us attractive or want a relationship with us. In that case, we will put that love letter in a safe place because we will want to go back and read it repeatedly. We find that written communication from the admirer to be exciting no matter

Ronald D. Walters

how many times we've read over it. However, the Christians who have the very Word of God at their disposal daily fail to pursue it because we no longer have any awe for the writer of the love letter. Our perception of our heavenly Father is that 'He is so controlling.' In our finite minds, we have lost the excitement of discovering what His infinite mind reveals in His Word, and we have become bored. We quickly move away from His Word and begin to trust the excitement of what the Bible calls "the world." 1 John 2:15 says, "Love not the world, neither the things in the world. If any man loves the world, the love of the Father is not in him." This verse does not mean that the Father stops loving as if God could become the "prodigal father" to spend all His love on those without deep relationships. More likely, we have become the prodigal lover and are bored with this God who paints a different sunrise every morning and brings a different sensation to our physical bodies through cold wind. The joy of warmth comes from the sun He created. Through the book of Revelation, John wrote that if we lose our "first love" for God and the joy of being surprised by God, He develops aught against us (Revelation 2:4).

Imposed social isolation will show us where our excitement in life lies and also what things excite us. When a Christian is born of water and spirit, there's awe and excitement about God's creations. We need to get more of his Word or His presence. Early in that relationship, we might even have had a prayer life. All this is because we were excited about this new relationship with a stable and sure God. I heard a wise preacher say that if something in your relationship with God has changed, it is not God!

Are you bored with marriage? You're probably bored with the giver of marriage and tired of child-rearing. You've lost your awe of God and no longer want to raise these children to serve a "boring" Lord. Not teaching your neighbors how much God loves them? You're allowing them to teach you how much excitement the world has. Let's fall in love with Jesus and never lose the surprise factor He wants to give us through His Word and daily actions.

If the world and the things of the world are where your excitement is, I recommend you divorce entertainment and remove your flirtation with lascivious and carnal pursuits. My dear friend, He shows His handiwork and lets us know He's on the way back. Remember, though! He's looking for a bride, an eternal lover. She is surprised by the beautiful sunrise painting and comforted in the warmth of brand-new mercy every day. Moving from where you rise after a night of sleep into a world that needs you to point out how awesome our heavenly lover is. Come on, Christian, you've got this.

Please read each of the following biblical examples in this lesson:

KEY VERSES

- "The fear [awe] of the Lord is the beginning of wisdom: and the knowledge of the holy is understanding." (Proverbs 9:10 KJV)
- "But unto you that fear [awe] my name shall the Sun of righteousness arise with healing in his wings; and ye shall go forth, and grow up as calves of the stall." (Malachi 4:2 KJV)
- "Let us hear the conclusion of the whole matter: Fear [awe] God, and keep his commandments: for this is the whole duty of man." (Ecclesiastes 12:13 KJV)
- "Praise ye the Lord. Blessed is the man that feareth [stand in awe] of the Lord, that delighteth greatly in his commandments." (Psalms 112:1 KJV)
- "O that there were such a heart in them, that they would fear [be in awe of] me, and keep all my commandments always, that it might be well with them, and with their children forever!" (Deuteronomy 5:29 KJV)

PRETHOUGHT

Overcome the world by staying excited for God!

NOTES

THE BOUNCE

DAY 9: EMOTION LESSON 8

ANTICIPATION

Prethought: Overlooking negative thought
makes anticipating happiness possible!

When you anticipate something, you think or do something about it before it happens. The feeling of anticipation helps us lead happier lives. A 2007 study by Van Boven and Ashworth compared the excitement people felt when looking forward to things or looking back at them. They asked participants to think about both past and future vacations. Overall, they measured more excitement when the participants thought about possible future vacations, because "We have an expectation that future events will make us feel more emotional than ones that have passed." We tend to talk more about things in the future we are excited about than things that have already happened.[15]

Neil Patel has three important psychological points about anticipation that can help us interact and understand others. First, Patel states that people anticipate happy experiences. Since the brain is always on, we cannot stop it from anticipating what's next. When anticipation happens, the brain receives a dopamine which stimulates happiness.

Research shows that our brains are designed to anticipate positive events. Second, our past experiences shape how we expect future events, also known as "perceptual anticipation." Research shows that stimuli are the cause, whether the results of past events, instructions on future tasks, or similarities between past and present events. Last, anticipation decreases when we're stressed. The brain tries to get rid of stress by adaptation or avoidance. Adapting to stress releases dopamine, which leads to feelings of happiness.[16]

The Pastor's Perspective

Hope: Let's take a last look at the earthly emotion of anticipation. Psychologists and professional marketers agree that anticipation deals with the hope that our subsequent experiences will be positive. They say that this mindset of anticipation comes from healthy past experiences. People constantly anticipating difficult, negative, or traumatic experiences can suffer from mental illness. Like any other part or system of the human body, the mind is subject to disease, contagions, and influences from outside our bodies; if the digestive system experiences a bug, we are ready to discharge everything we have eaten from the gut because the bug makes us feel sick. Developing a brain bug such as a painful or traumatic experience robs us of what the apostle wrote in Romans chapter 8: "We are saved by hope." Hope is the experience of joyous anticipation. It's challenging to live as Christ if we cannot ride in the saddle of hope since life moves to the left and the right and gives us ups and downs. If we don't have hope, we have no salvation because our strength is limited, and life's adversity destroys unstable faith. Unstable faith is what many Christians have, as they want to demand all life experiences to be positive. However, genuine faith means that regardless of life circumstances, I stay positive within the context of my being!

When killers of hope try to derail our positive experiences, we must remember the stories of suffering, pain, trauma, and other life experiences that true believers have endured because of hope.

Don't let your hope be destroyed; have faith, and be positive! Let your life be remade in Christ. As the Bible declares in Romans 8, we are saved by the joyous anticipation of a future in Heaven, where we shall reign with Christ! My hope is not in this world or the people of this world. My hope is in Christ. Therefore, I enjoy the fellowship of those of you who have found a life based on hope. Today, Christians endure real-life experiences and maintain a hopeful perspective; you will be saved and live happily!

KEY VERSES

- "For as many as are led by the Spirit of God, they are the sons of God. For ye have not received the spirit of bondage again to fear; but ye have received the Spirit of adoption, whereby we cry, Abba, Father. The spirit itself beareth witness with our spirit that we are the children of God: And if children, then heirs; heirs of God, and joint-heirs with Christ; if so be that we suffer with him, that we may also be glorified together. For I reckon that the sufferings of this present time are not worthy of being compared with the glory which shall be revealed in us. For the earnest expectation of the creature waiteth for the manifestation of the sons of God." (Romans 8:14-19 KJV)
- "And not only they, but ourselves also, which have the first fruits of the spirit, even we ourselves groan within ourselves, waiting for the adoption, to wit, the redemption of our body. For we are saved by hope: but hope that is seen is not hope: for what a man seeth, why doth he yet hope for?" (Romans 8:23-24 KJV)
- "If you faint on the day of adversity, your strength is small." (Proverbs 24:10)

PRETHOUGHT

My stability and joy come through Christ. My hope is in Jesus and him crucified!

Ronald D. Walters

NOTES

PART III

INTENTION

DAY 10: INTENTION LESSON 1

THINK DELIBERATELY; LIVE DELIGHTFULLY

Prethought: Think Deliberately; Live Delightfully

Dr. William Tiller states, "For the last four hundred years, an unstated assumption of science is that human intention cannot affect what we call 'physical reality.'" Experimental research of the past decade shows that, in today's world and under the right conditions, this assumption is no longer correct. We, humans, are much more than we think we are, and psychoenergetic science continues to expand the proof of it. Psychoenergetic refers to the power or force of mental/spiritual activity. In short, what we feel and how we purpose our thoughts, words, and actions cannot affect physical human reality.[17]

Tiller believes that our intentions can influence our physical surroundings. He developed crystal-based silicon that can collect the intentions directed by people in meditation. Their collective intentions resonate so highly that they can be widely broadcast to affect other people. Tiller has used this technology to change water pH by one point on the pH scale, grow larvae 30 percent faster, and kill bacteria 30 percent more quickly. We can see a connection between our intentions and our physical surroundings through Tiller's research. Science considers the spirit to be a proven side of self![18]

The Pastor's Perspective

Given the content of Dr. Tiller's article and writings, I continue to be amazed at the ability of science to catch up to the Word of God. A discussion of intent is essential to the believer who desires to be "effective" and is the centerpiece of living by faith. The above article demonstrates a scientific reference that shows that the mind of science is discovering that we have the power and authority to affect things around us by utilizing the energy that God has placed within us, which is a tremendous revelation that we, and the scientific community, finally understand what the Word of God stated millennia ago.

KEY VERSE

- "For the word of God is quick, powerful, and sharper than any two-edged sword, piercing even to the dividing asunder of soul and spirit, and the joints and marrow, and is a discerner of the thoughts and intents of the heart." (Hebrews 4:12 KJV)

KEY DEFINITION

- Intent - (intelligence, thought), intention, purpose.

INTENTIONS: EARTH TO GOD

- "If my people, called by my name, shall humble themselves, and pray, and seek my face, and turn from their wicked ways;

Ronald D. Walters

then will I hear from heaven, and will forgive their sin, and heal their land." (2 Chronicles 7:14 KJV)

INTENTIONS: GOD TO MAN

- "For the preaching of the cross is to them that perish foolishness; but unto us which are saved, it is the power of God. For it is written, I will destroy the wisdom of the wise and will bring to nothing the understanding of the prudent. Where is the wise? Where is the scribe? Where is the disputer of this world? Hath not God made foolish the wisdom of this world? For after that in the wisdom of God the world by wisdom knew not God, it pleased God by the foolishness of preaching to save them that believe." (1 Corinthians 1:18-31 KJV)

God designs the intent within the context of humanity to allow us to accomplish several essential protocols if we want to make Heaven our home! To presume that the experience of being "born again" through baptism and infilling of the Holy Ghost is all it takes for us to be Heaven-bound is irrational and self-serving.

Below are a few biblical references that relate to "intent." The first one is listed in Acts 10:29, a question Peter the apostle asked Cornelius at the birth of the Gentile church. The question is, "What is the intent?" The meeting between Peter and Cornelius and his family was supernaturally determined through Peter having a trance and Cornelius having a vision. This vision and trance indicate that somewhere in the intangible "spirit realm," there was a Heavenly intention manifest through human interaction that created a salvation experience for all those not fortunate enough to be the sons of Abraham.

- "Therefore came I unto you without gainsaying, as soon as I was sent for: I ask therefore for what <u>intent</u> ye have sent for me?" (Acts 10:29 KJV)

The second scriptural mention of intent that I've chosen comes from the book of Hebrews and shows us our troubles. It defines one of the reasons that we have a real problem with good biblical preaching. We subjectively choose the things we want to obey and the things we disobey by saying that "the preacher missed the interpretation of the scripture." We're saying that "I don't want God to use a preacher to reveal the real motivation for what I do." The writer of Hebrews indicates that the word of God is a discerner of the heart's intentions. A wife who says "I love you" to her husband as he leaves but intends to be angry and frustrated at him may have said the words, but "the heart's intention " differs from what was spoken. The Bible says that love does not hold grudges and does not think evil, yet we can utter, "I love you," with no

intention of being kind or generous with affection. Do not fear; the word of God discerns what you mean, and that is where we are measured.

A frustrated believer can say, "Well, God has too high expectations for me. Still, I have no intention of being Christian." Yeah, good preaching does provoke the evaluation of our

Ronald D. Walters

evil intentions. That's one of the reasons we don't turn away at the rebuke of the word of God or change behaviors to align accurately with His expectations because we have no 'intention' of changing.

The Word of God will reveal your heart's intentions! Say things you mean, and mean things that you say. Put action behind your words, and watch how intent changes the people and things around you. Then, your world will become a brighter place.

PRETHOUGHT

Anticipate that the Word of God, through good preaching, will cause correction, reproof, and instructions in being righteous.

NOTES

Ronald D. Walters

DAY 11: INTENTION LESSON 2

THINK WITH PURPOSE, LIVE WITH FULFILLMENT

Prethought: Think with Purpose, Live with Fulfillment

Intentionality is the act of being deliberate or purposive. Regarding philosophy, intentionality is defined as the quality of mental states directed toward some object or state of affairs.[19]

Many cultures have traditions about people who can heal the sick or injured without touching them or sometimes even being near them--known as Distance Healing Intention (DHI). Leonard Leibovici studied patients with bloodstream infections who were prayed for many years after they were diagnosed. The researchers wanted to know if DHI would work through time, not just physical space. Compared to the control group, who had received no prayer, the group who had received DHI had shorter hospital stays and were healthier. Dean Radin gathered studies on DHI and found that overall, DHI is the cause of increased health may seem like an illogical conclusion. The fact that the effects exist is, in principle, enough to believe.[20]

The Pastor's Perspective

Albert Einstein used the phrase "spooky stuff at a distance" to explain unexplainable things like energy between unrelated particles or life force. However, the power of intercessory prayer and its inexplicable ability to heal has boggled scientists for a long time. Science defines itself as the religion of man's mind, one in which man can take on a god-like quality. Indeed, man's mind created many modern devices like cell phones, plasma televisions, and light bulbs. Therefore, I need to be quicker to criticize the power of the scientific mind. Still, science has difficulty transitioning through the gulf of information, which proves that there is a greater force than us, yet it works within us. We, as Christians, know that the force is God.

John 1 tells us that He came to live with us, and His name is Jesus Christ. He accomplished many "mind-boggling" feats while walking the earth and left a legacy that we can choose to utilize or not.

Intention- The power behind the words we use, the actions we show, and the expressions on our faces as we interact. The intention is to bind together what is within us and express it toward someone or something outside of ourselves. According to scientists, it's 'spooky' how intention can affect objects and people around us.

KEY VERSE

- "For the word of God is quick, powerful, and sharper than any *twoedged* sword, piercing even to the dividing asunder of soul and spirit, and the joints and marrow, and is a discerner of the thoughts and intents of the heart." (Hebrews 4:12 KJV)

I hope that today we can live with intention. Draw together all your thoughts, energy, motivation, and feelings to project love and acceptance toward other people. Realize that intentional living can comfort and uplift those around us. We can have a positive or a negative effect on those around us. We can build someone up or tear them down in a 'spooky' distanced manner. I will pray for those around me that God will heal them and bless them. I'm going to start with myself. I intentionally move to my priority relationships, and I will move to love my neighbor. Jesus understood that we have power! Jesus said In Acts 1:8, "You shall receive power after that the Holy Ghost has come upon you, and you shall be witnesses" (KJV).

Let your total self be a witness to the value of other people, and enjoy building something worthwhile in those around you today. Those good people around you will satisfy the longing for closeness within you.

Prethought

By intending to influence those around me positively, the net result will positively affect me.

NOTES

Ronald D. Walters

THE BOUNCE

THINK AFFIRMATIONS

Prethought: Think Affirmations and live above your critics!

Within the context of Yoga, "sankalpa" is the concept of daily affirmations that lead to the belief that if we know what we want and regularly articulate it, we can use "magic" to manifest those desires into our lives. Now, this is not magic. It simply manipulates the mind's neuroplasticity or stretches it to believe differently. Psychiatrist Richard Davidson described how we're learning to shape our brains by changing our habits. The brain's neuroplasticity means it can restructure itself to solve the problem when we encounter new challenges. When we face the same challenge repeatedly, the neural pathways become smoother, and we solve the issues faster. Often, this occurs consciously, but we aren't aware of it most of the time. Davidson's team is researching the intentional training of the brain to improve well-being. Similarly, social psychologist Amy Cuddy has been studying how body language affects the mind, specifically how pretending to be powerful can make your body feel more powerful.[21]

Dr. William Tiller's research team has used science to prove the effects of the mind on the matter surrounding us. Specifically, they measured the change in electrical currents of objects exposed to intentional meditation. Tiller took four experienced meditators, each focused on an electrical device. That device was sent to a lab 2,000 miles away and placed next to a water container. The goal was to raise or lower the pH of the water by one whole unit simply by the proximity of the device and the intention of the meditation. Tiller's team measured a pH change of as much as 1½ units. Additionally, they discovered that the effect becomes permanent when an intentional meditation is repeated in one location. The pH change happened faster and in larger increments when the team repeated the experiment. Tiller said, "The alteration in the room's space has remained stable for over a year, and it's still going strong."[22]

The Pastor's Perspective

- "Now unto him, that can do exceedingly abundantly above all that we ask or think, according to the power that worketh in us, unto him be glory in the church by Christ Jesus throughout all ages, world without end. Amen." (Ephesians 3:20-21 KJV)

In the article referenced above, science proves that today's intentions create and reflect energy. Our meditations imprint the environment of our minds, body, and atmosphere of our homes. We create a hostile environment if we focus on violent and evil thoughts. We will create an energy that reflects these meditations. If we chose positive reviews, we would have a positive environment.

Some would say, "Well, I did not intend to think this way, but the other person caused me to be angry, seditious, evil speaking, less than loving, and not encouraging." Then, they feel justified in not controlling their 'inner self.' I am sorry, but this excuse is lame and quite lazy. Let's be Christian and live scientifically. As a challenge, try controlling your personal space via intentional positive thinking. Immediately self-talk good things—don't wait another minute! Do not let one more negative intention settle in your brain, or it might slip out of your mouth.

Remember that the way you intend to think is like a thermostat in your body and will affect the atmosphere in your room. Your intentions influence your environment and those around you. Make this your daily creed: "Today, I intend to love those close to me through Word and action. I intend to accept all of those around me, even if they can hurt me. If my intention to help them is strong enough, I shall have an effect because of my intentions."

To be blunt, don't think insensitive and angry thoughts. They will only generate a stupefied, enraged environment around you and destroy the people that must endure your mind. Those thoughts hinder the joy, peace, and pleasure you will have throughout the day. According to the reference above, it may even change the pH of the water near you.

In John 7:38, Jesus reports, "He that believeth on me, as the scripture hath said, out of his belly shall flow rivers of living water." Our intentions determine the warmth of that flow.

KEY VERSE

- "Blessed is the man that walketh not in the counsel of the ungodly, nor standeth in the way of sinners, nor sitteth in the seat of the scornful. But his delight is in the law of the Lord; and in his law doth he meditate day and night. And he shall be like a tree planted by the rivers of water, that bringeth forth his fruit in his season; his leaf also shall not wither; and whatsoever he doeth shall prosper. The ungodly are not so: but are like the chaff which the wind driveth away. Therefore the ungodly shall not stand in judgment, nor sinners in the congregation of the righteous. For the Lord knoweth the way of the righteous: but the way of the ungodly shall perish." (Psalm 1:1-6 KJV)

"Now unto him, that can do exceedingly abundantly above all that we ask or think, according to the power that worketh in us, unto him be glory in the church by Christ Jesus throughout all ages, world without end. <u>Prethought:</u> I intend to warm those around me by keeping a positive, warm intention.

Ronald D. Walters

NOTES

THOUGHT DISCIPLINE

Prethought: With disciplined thought,
my battles are already fought!

Researchers at Stanford University studied endurance during exercise and feeling full while eating. The researchers tested participants for a gene that makes a person more or less prone to tiring. They were then asked to run on a treadmill before being randomly divided into two groups. One group was told they had the gene, and the other did not. The participants were then asked to run on the treadmill again. Those who were told they had the tiring gene didn't run as long as they had before, while those who were told they had the better endurance gene ran longer than they had in the first part of the study, which occurred regardless of the actual genetic results.[23]

Ronald D. Walters

The Pastor's Perspective

In the world of human existence through the lens of Christianity, there are naturally two groups of people. The first group has been born into a world known to be fallen and where they only hear dark things. In this dark world, people are predators, abusers, destructive, go about carnally, and have the capability of hurting each other. This darkness comes naturally and doesn't need any advanced teaching, according to Isaiah 60:1-2.

KEY VERSE

- "Arise, shine; for thy light is come, and the glory of the Lord is risen upon thee. For, behold, the darkness shall cover the earth, and gross darkness the people: but the Lord shall arise upon thee, and his glory shall be seen upon thee." (Isaiah 60:1-2 KJV)

This dark world is a place where flesh rules, and it is every man or every woman for themselves. This pursuit of carnality shows that no one is safe from potential harm.

In the dark world of carnality, people attempt to dispose of the proof of their choices and actions. We get married and ruin the relationship through the pursuit of selfishness. Then, we try to cover the evidence of it through a divorce. When we become physically intimate with a member of the opposite gender, a seed begins growing, and we hide reality through abortion. We are the victims of other people's terrible treatment. We try to cover the proof held within our memories by becoming dependent on alcohol or drugs. We are victimized in childhood by bullies, and we become wrath-filled and belligerent to conceal our vulnerabilities.

In Galatians, chapter 5, the works of the flesh are described as adultery, fornication, wrath, strife, sedition, heresy, envy, murder, drunkenness, and reveling, which happen when people have only heard that you have the carnal gene and were 'born that way.' A second group on the earth has learned that they don't have to live according to the rules of darkness. They don't have to abuse one another, and they don't have to seek only what is suitable for themselves. This group is the body of Christ! We, who are part of his church, are so fortunate! When we come out of the waters of baptism after repenting, we begin to 'hear' that we have new genes (we have a new father). In the way we used to live our lives, we were destroyers, but now we come into the body of Christ. Then suddenly, "Faith comes by hearing and hearing by the word of God," and we recognize the sound of new life. When we get on the treadmill of existence, we suddenly have more endurance, less capacity for sin, and more desire to build the people around us.

The first group has no hope because all they hear is the world's entertainment, music, and stories of despair and pandemics. However, in the second study group, the body of Christ, we have learned to conform to a world that is not a part of the darkness. Our Lord empowered us when He said, "You are the light of the world" (Matthew 5:14). Also, the Lord said, "Nothing shall be impossible to you" (Matthew 17:20).

According to the study of human nature, you will become what you've heard you can be. You believe the report of the things you're listening to and the words you're hearing. Then, the sad continuation of this reality is that I have made the people around me become what I have said they are. How about we develop the body image of Heaven by becoming loving, and peace-giving, seeking satisfaction for other people, serving one another with love, and creating within the sphere of influence a reality that is the result of "the preaching of the cross."

Ronald D. Walters

The single most significant moment in all eternity was when Jesus Christ made it to the cross without sin, so we could hear that we've got an opportunity to choose a new dad, our Father in Heaven, who gives us the genes of love.

PRETHOUGHT

I am the world's light, and the darkness has no hold on me. Therefore, I will think light toward all men.

NOTES

Ronald D. Walters

MELODY OF INTENTION

Prethought: Listening to intention's happy
melody brings complete peace to me!

The power of intent can be seen in some parts of Africa, where mothers write and sing songs for their children while pregnant. Then, when the mother is not within earshot of their crying child, they sense the child's distress and sing the song. The child, in return, senses the mother's song and calms themselves. This is true even in business. If a CEO or manager asks for feedback from their team but does not plan to use it, the team will not be honest. Most people can easily perceive the intentions of those around them.[24]

Einstein once observed what he called "spooky action at a distance." More modern research on physics has named this concept: entanglement and non-locality. In physics, entanglement occurs when two particles are so wholly connected that they cannot be affected separately, even if they are nowhere near each other. We can see this phenomenon outside of science in our relationships. For example, if you suddenly think about a friend you haven't seen in a while, then they call you, that's quantum entanglement. Similarly, twins often know what the other is thinking or feeling. This phenomenon has been known in society as "twin telepathy" but is another example of quantum entanglement.[25]

Modern science has assumed that human intention does not affect reality. Dr. William Tiller's research shows the exact opposite. His team is discovering how "we humans are much more than we think we are." Psychoenergetic science continues to expand the proof of it.[26]

The Pastor's Perspective

You are at this point in your life exactly where you have thought yourself to be!

According to Harvard Business School and Albert Einstein, intent provides influence even from a distance!

Unto me, who am less than the least of all saints, is this grace given, that I should preach among the Gentiles the unsearchable riches of Christ; and to make all men see what is the fellowship of the mystery, which from the beginning of the world hath been hid in God, who created all things by Jesus Christ: to the intent that now unto the principalities and powers in heavenly places might be known by the church

Ronald D. Walters

the manifold wisdom of God, according to the eternal purpose which He purposed in Christ Jesus our Lord: in whom we have boldness and access with confidence by the faith of him. Wherefore I desire that ye faint not at my tribulations for you, which is your glory. Paul wrote about the power of intent long before the scientists understood that it was even subject matter to be considered. Paul preached with intention, and the church can hear and, by reflection, implement our Creator's strategies (powerful intent) through obedience to biblical mandates.

The research cited above shows that the right intention can create and grow a business. Moreover, a mother who intends to please her child can do so, even from a distance, beyond the physical ability of the child to hear her voice, just because she intends to comfort the baby. What if we took the science of intent and coupled that with the intention of the Word of God?

Obedience to the principles of God's Word allows the intention of a God who becomes so far away the reality of where we live, within close confinement of other human beings around us.

Consider the effect that this could have on:

1. Your spouse - What if we intended to ensure that our spouses were equipped with the highest level of loving intent? What if I focused on my love for and for my spouse today? According to science, I can provide my spouse with comfort and unconditional support from a distance. Could this be why the apostle Paul said, "Husbands love your wife and wives submit yourselves to your husband[s]?" (Ephesians 2:22). Unless we "intend" to give it a spin, we'll never know. Our marriages are precisely where we thought they would be. Do you want your spouse to be more successful? Then, through the power of intention, believe that it's happening, and it will happen.

2. Your children - Take to heart the description of what happens in the African community, where the mother intends to soothe

her child by conditioning the child's mind within the context of a particular song written with the intention of a loving mother. Could our children be exactly where their parents have nurtured them to be in the world and in Christ? Their ability to learn, implement, strategize for life, engage others in relationships, and rise to the challenge of being a Christian requires them to reflect our intentions as a parent. That may be why in the book of Deuteronomy, the Word tells us to teach these principles daily and place them like frontlets between the eyes and as a signet on our hands.

3. The church culture - What if I stopped judging others according to my insecurities and interpreting their values by how they appear on the outside? Could it be that if I intend to love my brothers and sisters, my love will, even from a distance, affect how the church culture grows? I am responsible for keeping a clean heart, having a ready mind, and pouring into my brothers and sisters. Mark my words, it will all be sorted out when you stand in that white throne room, and your actions and words will bring judgment, not to the target of my judgement, but to me as I am now the target. Your words and actions have painted on your soul as seen in Matthew 7:1-2.

4. The world around us- I am commanded to have good intentions toward myself and my neighbors. Jesus thought all the law and the prophets should hang on to one idea. To love God with all my heart, soul, mind, and strength, and I would love my neighbor as I love myself. It is a tragedy for those who can't love themselves enough to reach someone outside our small circles and extend love. We may deserve judgment and could receive it at the hands of inactivity and unwillingness to teach anyone around us about the love of God that should be within us. We are whited sepulchers, beautiful outside but dead inside. We unknowingly prepare ourselves for an eternity away from the God who intended us to be so much more in this world.

How many of us have cursed the fig tree of our lives? Our judgment and condemnation of others have returned to our lives and are raining the fruit of the vine. Jesus said faith was released, and what was become of the fig tree was a fruitless death to the roots (Matthew 21:19-22). Many of us have done this to our marriages and our children. By not sharing the Word with those around you, you've allowed your neighbors to continue to live in darkness, all because you intended to do that very thing!

What hope do those around us have if the power within us intends to do nothing? If I intend to do nothing, the results shall be seen. Now, without hesitation, decide to intentionally affect your mind by thinking positive thoughts about what you can become. Make it your intention to be what He has called you to be: a tree of love, peace, joy, temperance, long-suffering, goodness, and faithfulness.

With intention, ask God to bless those around you and even repent for how you have influenced people up to this point in your life. Call out to God for His mercy, and He will hear you and allow you the opportunity to have a second chance at love. Let's stop ruining people and allow the Lord to build us into the temple He's called us to be. A beautiful place where love is not only shown but also released through intention into a dark world so desperately needs this light. Thus, be the solution God wants you to be.

KEY VERSE

- "Now unto him that is able to do exceeding abundantly above all that we ask or think, according to the power that worketh in us, unto him be glory in the church by Christ Jesus throughout all ages, world without end. Amen." (Ephesians 3:8-21 KJV)
- "Jesus answered and said unto them, Verily I say unto you, If ye have faith, (intention) and doubt not, ye shall not only do this which is done to the fig tree, but also if ye shall say unto this mountain, Be thou removed, and be thou cast into the sea; it

shall be done. And all things, whatsoever ye shall ask in prayer, believing, ye shall receive." (Matthew 21:21-22 KJV)

PRETHOUGHT

I will prepare to make a difference by becoming the difference I want to make. Love improves all things, and I will use it generously.

Ronald D. Walters

NOTES

THE BOUNCE

CHOOSE GOOD INTENTIONS, LIVE GOOD RELATIONSHIPS

Prethought: Choose Good Intentions, Live Good Relationships

Richard Gordon believes most modern scientists do not look at psychic phenomena because they believe the world functions mechanically. However, Gordon has gathered multiple studies that show the power of the mind. Gordon discussed Dr. Tiller's study on DHI raising the pH of water. Dean Radin performed an analysis and found that a person observing photons traveling through slits can affect the photon's path. Lynn McTaggart performed an experiment where 10,000 people from eighty countries focused their mental energy on influencing a single leaf to glow brighter than a leaf that received no attention.[27]

Ronald D. Walters

Earl Nightingale developed the concept of "The Strangest Secret." The secret is why some people are successful while others are not. According to Nightingale, only 5 percent of men aged sixty-five and older have achieved the financial success for which they had hoped. However, do 95 percent of people fail at their goals? To find the answer, Nightingale defined success as "the progressive realization of a worthy ideal." Therefore, success is relative to each person. Success does not have to be financial; it simply does whatever job you've always wanted. Nightingale says many people 'fail' because they conform to society and act like everyone else without discovering themselves. The one concept that all wise thinkers through history agree on is this: we become what we think about most.[28]

The Pastor's Perspective

For each of us, our happiness, satisfaction with life, marriage, parenting experiences, business life, cash flow, and acquired assets is a very telling story read by all. The investment of our time and experiences we have had have all been meticulously authored by the thoughts that each of us has allowed into our mind and which have become who we are! As typical of science, if you dig deep enough, you see that many of their experiments are deliberately set in motion by the Lord God Almighty to confirm His word. In the investigation, "A Focused Intent," the designer of the test chose two leaves. One of the leaves was the target of people worldwide, thinking positively that the leaf would "glow." In the controlled environment of that experiment, the leaf that was considered positive indeed "glowed much brighter" than the leaf that was ignored.

The prophetic power of David was that the example written in Psalms 1 indicates that if we meditate on God's law (intention), we receive all of the positive thoughts of Heaven. We become the leaf (life) that eternity chose to ignite glowing power on this earth. Think of the concepts of our Lord as related through the authors of the gospels:

"If you love me, keep my Commandments" (established thought), "You are the light of the world" (glowing influence) (John 14:15, Matthew 5:14). In other words, you are the glowing leaf who demonstrates the focus thoughts of Heaven that we will shine. Think of the prophet Isaiah, "Arise and shine for the latest come, and the glory of the Lord is risen upon Thee" (Isaiah 60:1).

It is my personal choice to disengage from negative thoughts which, in turn, frees me to engage in positive thought. By having a positive paradigm, I can be thankful that the word teaches me that outside of obedience to God's word, I am a sinner. This then gives me a positive approach to repenting of my sin. Then I become glad that the word revealed to me that starting with the precious corner stone in Zion, there's a name wherein I can find remission of my sin. I'm thankful that the Word told me I was a sinner, so I could genuinely repent of my sin! I'm glad that what was revealed to me, starting with the precious stone in Zion. , was that there is a name wherein I could be baptized for the remission of sin. I am also thankful that it was shown to me that I could receive the power of the Holy Ghost with the evidence of Heaven speaking, through me, the tongues of men and angels! I'm also thankful that it didn't leave me as a newborn babe but gave me an opportunity for daily and eternal instruction in what Heaven determined is righteousness.

The truth is that your marriage is what you thought it would be, your children will grow to be exactly as you think they should, your finances are precisely what you want, and your friendships on earth are just as valuable as you've made them. Hey, Word to the wise on this beautiful day: stop being unrealistic, negative, and the sole determiner of your misery. Take the apostles as an example. Rise and walk in a new life with Christ. Be a glowing leaf. Start thinking about something you want to become and watch how your thoughts usher you into that new reality. Not because science is so bad, but because long before scientists ever discovered this idea, the Word of God had established it from the foundation of the world. His name is Jesus, by the way! In the words of Gerry Goffin and Carole King, "Will you still love me tomorrow?" Hopefully, you will hear the melody of love as you pursue "leaf!" Get it,

Ronald D. Walters

pursue "leaf?" Pursue life thinking positive thoughts. Glow and become what you've always wanted to be. You can do it!

KEY VERSE

- "Blessed is the man that walketh not in the counsel [principles of thought] of the ungodly, nor standeth in the way of sinners, [those adhering to Adamic indulgence of rebellion to the Words of God] nor sitteth in the seat of the scornful [Embittered embittered mockers of life in Christ]. But his delight is in the law of the Lord, and in His law doth he meditate meditates day and night. And he shall be like a tree planted by the rivers of water, that bringeth forth his fruit in his season; his leaf also shall not wither; and whatsoever he doeth shall prosper. The ungodly are not so: but are like the chaff which the wind driveth away. Therefore, the ungodly shall not stand in judgment nor sinners in the congregation of the righteous. For the Lord knoweth the way of the righteous: but the way of the ungodly shall perish." (Psalm 1:1-6 KJV)

NOTES

THE BOUNCE

THINK STRENGTH; LIVE STRONG

Prethought: Think Strength; Live Strong

Brian Clark and his colleagues wanted to test the brain's influence on strength development. They designed a four-week study in which fourteen people wore a cast on their arm that immobilized their wrist and hand. Fifteen additional people did not have casts. The ones who had the cast were asked to perform mental imagery exercises five times a week to imagine that they were moving the immobilized wrist. The other fourteen did no exercises. After four weeks, the group who did not perform the exercises had 45 percent less strength than the control group. The group who completed the exercises had 25 percent less strength. Clark believes this study shows the effect our brain alone can have on our physical body. The experiment results demonstrate that when they thought right, even without physical exercise, the participants maintained strength.[29]

The Pastor's Perspective

The word "strength" occurs 232 in the Bible. It is mentioned in 39 of the 66 books and shows up repeatedly in Psalms 70, Isaiah 33, and Job 22.

KEY VERSE

- "For this, cause I bow my knees unto the Father of our Lord Jesus Christ, Of whom the whole family in Heaven and earth is named, That he would grant you, according to the riches of his glory, to be strengthened with might by his Spirit in the inner man; That Christ may dwell in your hearts by faith; that ye, being rooted and grounded in love, May be able to comprehend with all saints what is the breadth, and length, and depth, and height; And to know the love of Christ, which passeth knowledge, that ye might be filled with all the fullness of God. Now unto him, that can do exceeding abundantly above all that we ask or think, according to the power that worketh in us, Unto him be glory in the church by Christ Jesus throughout all ages, world without end. Amen." (Ephesians 3:14-21 KJV)

In the verse above, Paul indicates that strength is fostered within us. He begins this writing in the posture of a "bended knee," which means prayer to and meditation on God. We are to be "strengthened" with might by His spirit in the inner man.

Ronald D. Walters

Fear, jealousy, and envy are all spiritual immobilizers and stem from a belief that something terrible will happen in the inner man. When fear hits us, we tend to recoil and not do anything. Then we meditate on how scary life is and consequently do nothing. In a way, we are in a "lifecast" where we do nothing. We then complain that we have nothing.

The solution to this mental sickness is to stop letting fear immobilize your love. Begin to use your imagination, think positively through this immobilization, and watch how God establishes steps for you. It is not God's will that you remain motionless or in an effortless place because you're afraid to move. Think of all the good that will come into your life if you release the strength of the inner person where the Spirit of the living God resides! Just thinking right will cause you to maintain the strength you didn't even know you had.

Whatever part of your life is gripped by fear and needs improvement, begin to think positive thoughts about it. Then, watch how God establishes a brand-new day for you! Marriages, parenting, and friendships can all be blessed if we imagine those relationships healthy and prosperous. Remember what David said in Psalm 1, "But his delight is in the law of the Lord and in his law does he meditate both day and night. He shall be like a tree planted by the water. Everything he does shall prosper" (KJV).

Meditation is simply mental imaging, and if we allow that imaging focus on seeing the love of God, we have a greater potential to bring the prosperity of heaven into our earthly life. A positive mental imaging on the love of God allows my relationships to be potentially stronger than if I imagined the to be sad. If I follow the same logic in my finances and in my parenting, as an example, it will stand to reason that each of these important roles will be a more positive experience for me. It stands to reason that if I can imagine myself as a happier person, it will impact the level of love I show to my spouse as well as everything else in my life. If I think right, I will experience strength and be able to live right! Your relationships are stronger than you imagined. In the same case, your finances are more powerful than you imagined! Now, imagine yourself being happier, and you will be more in love with your spouse. You will be a more effective, powerful parent. All of this is possible because just by thinking strength into your person. Think right, and you will experience strength!

Pre-thought

Mold the way you feel by realizing personal strength is real.

Ronald D. Walters

NOTES

THE BOUNCE

DAY 17: INTENTION LESSON 8

INTENTIONAL MEDITATION; PERSONAL SATISFACTION

Prethought: If I use intentional meditation, I will secure personal satisfaction!

Mindful meditation is an essential tool for mental health. Gaëlle Desbordes's research uses fMRI (functional magnetic resonance imaging), which scans the brain by taking and recording pictures. Specifically, Desbordes's 2012 research showed that people who meditate have more continuous brain activity than those who don't meditate. Desbordes scanned participants for over two months during everyday tasks, before and after meditation. The scans detected slight changes in activity in the amygdala, the part of

Ronald D. Walters

the brain associated with emotion. Previously, no activity changes were recorded in the amygdala. Desbordes's more recent research used fMRI technology to scan the brains of clinically depressed patients. During the scan, patients were directed to practice mindful meditation, meditating on a series of phrases such as "I am such a loser" or "I can't go on." After a couple of minutes, the patients were asked to stop ruminating, and the researchers measured how quickly the patients' brains disengaged from negative phrases. In the 1970s, Professor Herbert Benson developed "The Relaxation Response" as the commonality between meditation, yoga, and religious prayer. Benson described this response as the opposite of the "fight or flight" response.[30]

The Pastor's Perspective

Are you repeating self-chatter using phrases like: "I am such a loser," "I can't go on," "My kids are frustrating," "I need to leave my marriage," "My job is my problem," "My spouse is my problem," or "My friends are my problem"? According to science, these are phrases used by people who are clinically depressed. You could be repeating and chattering with those negative self-phrases because you are your problem. More specifically, the way we think is our problem. If this is you, do not make any major decisions right now. Please do not make any massive life changes because you will regret them. In other words, if you make a significant life decision while depressed without getting help, you will regret it when your mind finally comes back to normal.

KEY VERSES

- "And God saw that the wickedness of man was great in the earth and that every imagination of the thoughts of his heart was only evil continually." (Genesis 6:5 KJV)
- "And be not conformed to this world: but be ye transformed by the renewing of your mind, that ye may prove what is that good, and acceptable, and perfect, will of God." (Romans 12:2 KJV)

- "For to be carnally minded is death; but to be spiritually minded is life and peace." (Romans 8:6 KJV)
- "For who hath known the mind of the Lord, that he may instruct him? But we have the mind of Christ." (1 Corinthians 2:16 KJV)
- "In whom the god of this world hath blinded the minds of them which believe not, lest the light of the glorious gospel of Christ, who is the image of God, should shine unto them." (2 Corinthians 4:4 KJV)
- "Casting down imaginations, and every high thing that exalteth itself against the knowledge of God, and bringing into captivity every thought to the obedience of Christ;" (2 Corinthians 10:5 KJV)
- "But I fear, lest by any means, as the serpent beguiled Eve through his subtlety, so your minds should be corrupted from the simplicity that is in Christ." (2 Corinthians 11:3 KJV)
- "And be renewed in the spirit of your mind;" (Ephesians 4:23 KJV)
- "And you, that were sometime alienated and enemies in your mind by wicked works, yet now hath he reconciled." (Colossians 1:21 KJV)

The beauty of science is that it constantly confirms what God's Word has stated for thousands of years. God has plans for us, and if we live the patterns of His book, The Bible, we will enjoy the results of his plans. He is an architect/ master builder trying to help you build a life worth living. In the article above, the facts science disclose about the brain demonstrate the word of God. If we can learn to think and meditate on the word of God, our meditation will cause a change in the literal substance of our brain. Why spend a lifetime struggling with depression and anxiety when it is as easy as allowing the word of your Creator to show you how to change your thoughts? To not allow the word of God to change your life, you

Ronald D. Walters

must be either unwilling (rebellion) or unable, which would require that you cannot understand what I'm writing.

He has a beautiful life for you, free of addiction, anger, and destructive relationship patterns, so heed the word of God. Obey what comes forth from that word in the form of preaching. It is not about finding happiness. Living for the idea of happiness leads to walking in the counsel of the ungodly, standing in the way with sinners, and allowing ourselves to sit in the seat of the bitter.

Now take a moment, and begin thinking about your closest human relationship, whether a spouse, a child, or—if you are utterly alone in this world—just a relationship with yourself. Think happy and loving thoughts about that person you have identified. Hold onto those warm, loving thoughts, and watch how your brain will begin to think such thoughts about everything in your day. I don't need a yoga instructor or any therapeutic intervention if I focus on God's word and meditate on it all day and night. This approach may work for you too, but you will only know once you try. I believe in you and in the power of God, His Word, and its ability to change our thinking. We can all reach a place of mindfulness and intentionality that pleases the Lord and gives us the greatest and happiest human experience while we walk this earth.

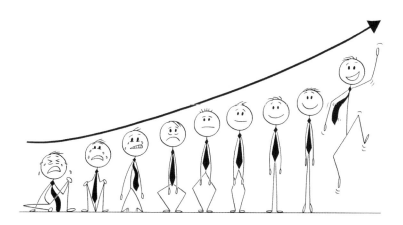

NOTES

Ronald D. Walters

PART IV

HATRED

DAY 18: HATRED LESSON 1

OVERVIEW OF HATRED

Prethought: I will daily release thoughts that
are bad and be the best me that I can be!

Psychologist Allison Abrams reviewed numerous studies and explored the factors that explain hate, including fear of self, fear of others, and lack of self-compassion. Abrams notes that hate also fills a void of societal and cultural factors. Psychologist Patrick Wanis believes that hatred can be caused by love for things that we know and relate to or by aggression toward things that are different or seen as a threat. Psychologist Dana Harron argues that hatred can manifest from our fears of something inside ourselves and that we then project that fear onto another person or object. Freud explained projection as rejecting what we don't like about ourselves. Psychologist Bernard Golden believes that hating a group of people is a way to avoid finding one's own identity and that we must be taught to hate others. Hatred is not a natural response to things. Psychologist Brad Reedy believes we desire to be good, so we project our own "badness" onto something else that we can attack because we worry our negative traits will cause others to reject us and we will end up alone.[31]

Therefore, we typically hate simply due to the fear of different things. The best way to avoid hate is to have compassion for others and ourselves. We will not judge others if we genuinely accept every part of ourselves.[32] [28]

The Pastor's Perspective

Understanding the effects of hatred is an integral part of the building blocks of truly Christian life—one that allows each believer to coexist with others while walking through our human experience. In this chapter, we examine some critical scriptural references found in the writings of Solomon, and many other scriptures defining and confining hatred, to expose its long-lasting effects that can affect us.

Acknowledging that hatred is possible in humans may motivate us to rid ourselves of this destructive process. Acknowledging that not only is God capable of hate but that He manifests it toward individuals helps us understand why we need to rid ourselves of this emotional plague. It would be great to be free of hatred toward yourself and others before you stand before God in His throne room of judgment. I look forward to discussing the changes He can make within us through dispelling hatred and, consequently, within the confines of a happier church; this will provide a happier you. We can learn to love others as we love ourselves. Living on this earth with hatred, variance, or even the slightest dislike for other human beings while here wastes your time and could also put you in the lake of fire for all of eternity. Consider these personal traits and keep these verses in mind as we begin our study.

KEY VERSE

- "These six things doth the Lord hate: yea, seven are an abomination unto him: A proud look, a lying tongue, and hands that shed innocent blood. A heart that deviseth wicked imaginations, feet that be swift in the running to mischief, A false witness that speaketh lies, and he that soweth discord among brethren." (Proverbs 6:16-19 KJV)

KJV DICTIONARY DEFINITION FOR HATE

Hate

Transitive verb. To dislike greatly; to have a great aversion to. It expresses less than abhor, detest, and abominate unless pronounced with a peculiar emphasis.

IN SCRIPTURE, IT MEANS TO LOVE LESS

Hate: noun. Great dislike or aversion; hatred.

Hated: past participle. Greatly disliked.

Hateful: adjective, odious; exciting great dislike, aversion, or disgust. Example: all sin is hateful in the sight of God and good men. That feels hatred, malignant, malevolent.

Hatefulness: noun. Odiousness; is the quality of being hateful or eliciting aversion or disgust.

Hating: verb. Disliking immensely; entertaining a strong aversion for.

NOTES

Ronald D. Walters

THE BOUNCE

EMPHASIS ON "A PROUD LOOK."

Prethought: If I decide to be proud,
it's an unhealthy shroud!

Pride has two primary meanings. The first is "a feeling that you respect yourself and deserve to be respected by others." The other is "a feeling that you are more important or better than others." The first definition is a healthy aspect of pride necessary for good self-esteem. In contrast, the second causes excessive pride in oneself. We need healthy pride to have stability in how much we value ourselves as individuals, regardless of our achievements. Those with an overinflated sense of pride often repel those around them because they do not see others as equally valuable as themselves. These people are typically overcompensating for their lack of self-pride. Pride can even prevent us from seeing our wrongdoings. Rather than being filled with an overinflated sense of pride, we need to have dignity in ourselves and others as human beings.[33]

Joan Cyril Abello lays out eleven signs of an overinflated sense of pride that you can use to evaluate yourself. Pay attention to the motivations behind what you are doing and thinking.

1. You think you are humble.
2. You do not accept constructive criticisms.
3. You always want to be the center of attention.
4. You are vain about your physical appearance.
5. You do not like associating with the "ordinary" or unpopular.
6. You are fond of name-dropping.
7. You are not teachable.
8. You do not listen to others' advice.
9. You are critical of those who have the potential to do better than you.
10. You think you are too important to do mundane things.
11. You do not like to be surpassed by anyone.[34]

The Pastor's Perspective

The six things the Lord hates begin with the concept of a "proud look." Since all things in The Word have deeper meanings, we understand that all concepts discussed in the canonized scripture have external and internal meanings. Keep this in mind as Solomon describes the building blocks of becoming a biblical abomination. We should pay close attention to how we are given a picture of things we don't want to be.

Remember, the idea of a proud look in the context given above means having low self-esteem on the inside but wanting to appear high, super important, and better than others on the outside. When you look inside, through the eyes of man and the world, you see very little, so you must try to act big when you look outside. Scripture defined this distorted look as the beginning of an unfruitful life, which leads to a destructive end.

Ronald D. Walters

In Deuteronomy chapter 6, Moses tries to help us understand the great concept of God and the importance of loving Him with all of our heart, soul, and strength. If we could adopt this positive pattern in our life, we would not have trouble loving and caring for the people around us. When we do not have a great sense of ourselves, seeing ourselves through the eyes of God, there is no way to have a proper understanding of seeing the value in others. This outcome is one of the effects of being conceited.

Since we have nothing to offer on the inside, we can judge everyone around us.

Remember, our God is an architect, and Solomon shows us how the things we genuinely do not want to build into our lives. Pride can be defined as the epitome of laziness. If I have low self-worth, there is little hope that I will engage others by serving them.

KEY VERSES

- "When pride cometh, then cometh shame: but with the lowly is wisdom." (Proverbs 11:2 KJV)
- "The fear of the Lord is to hate evil: pride, and arrogancy, and the evil way, and the froward mouth, do I hate." (Proverbs 8:13 KJV)
- "Be of the same mind one toward another. Mind not high things, but condescend to men of low estate. Be not wise in your own conceits." (Romans 12:16 KJV)
- "A man's pride shall bring him low: but honor shall uphold the humble in spirit." (Proverbs 29:23 KJV)
- "But the Lord said unto Samuel, look not on his countenance, or on the height of his stature; because I have refused him: for the Lord seeth not as man seeth; for man looketh on the outward appearance, but the Lord looketh on the heart." (1 Samuel 16:7 KJV)

- "But he that glorieth, let him glory in the Lord. For not he that commendeth himself is approved, but whom the Lord commendeth." (2 Corinthians 10:17-18 KJV)
- "Before destruction the heart of man is haughty, and before honor is humility." (Proverbs 18:12 KJV)
- "And he said That which cometh out of the man, that defileth the man. For from within, out of the heart of men, proceed evil thoughts, adulteries, fornications, murders, Thefts, covetousness, wickedness, deceit, lasciviousness, an evil eye, blasphemy, pride, foolishness: All these evil things come from within, and defile the man." (Mark 7:20-23 KJV)

Let's kick pride to the curb! Serve the Lord by studying His word and thinking the right thoughts about other people. Practice being humble by doing the things that humility calls us to do. First, begin with the Lord, by proclaiming his Lordship over your life. Let this humility become the drawing power of God that others see in you. Allowing this change to happen in you means that you don't have to be correct or superior; you can rejoice with those who rejoice, because humility causes you to weep with those who weep. Begin with your closest earthly relationship, whether that is a spouse or other meaningful and life-giving connection. Enter that relationship today with humility, and humility and show the other person how valuable they are by demonstrating how valuable you are in the eyes of God.

Ronald D. Walters

NOTES

THE BOUNCE

EMPHASIS ON "A LYING TONGUE."

Prethought: In order to live well, never a lie will I tell!

As we consider the following list of things that the culture sees as lying, it becomes clear why the Lord hates a lying tongue. Jesus described himself as "the way, the truth, and the life." Anything less than that is living below the blessings he has called us to live within. These blessings are available when we live within the confines of "truth!" This list is lengthy but not all-encompassing.

- A lie is a false statement that is used to deceive others. Different types of lies can be used for many various reasons.
- A bare-faced lie describes clearly incorrect information to the hearer.
- A big lie is a lie of considerable magnitude.
- A blue lie is done for the greater good.
- A bluff is a lie suggesting one has something they really do not.
- B.S. is a lie that the speaker may not even believe themselves but is said to give the hearer a specific impression.
- A cover-up is used to hide a previous lie or action.
- Defamation is a lie that hurts the reputation of someone else.
- Deflecting is avoiding the subject of the lie.

Ronald D. Walters

- Disinformation is intentionally spreading false information.
- An exaggeration is a lie where most of the person's words are accurate but only up to a certain point.
- Fake News is lies spread by news media outlets.
- A fib is a lie that is easy to forgive.
- Fraud is a lie used for financial gain.
- A half-truth only has part of the truth.
- Jocose lies are understood within the group to be teasing and humorous.
- A lie-to-children occurs when we oversimplify what we tell children.
- Lying by omission is when most truth is told, but critical facts are left out.
- Lying in trade is when a company advertises false information about its products.
- A memory hole is a lie where someone edits documents or photos to remove something from existence.
- Minimization is a lie where aspects are toned down to deny them.
- Mutual deceit is a lie wanted by both the speaker and the hearer.
- A noble lie is told to maintain law and order.
- Pathological lying is consistent and compulsive behavior.
- Perjury occurs when a person lies under oath in court or an official sworn statement.
- A polite lie may be needed depending on the speaker's or hearer's culture.
- Puffery is an exaggerated claim that cannot be proven false.
- Speaking with a forked tongue means that a person is hypocritical in what they say and does.
- Lastly, a white lie is seen as harmless by the speaker.[35]

How many kinds of lies have you told?

The Pastor's Perspective

Lying is procreative, meaning that lying once leads to other lies. We see that lying had a father as we have read the scriptural premise in John chapter 8. The procreator of all liars is defined by scripture as "Satan." Psychologists have popularized the statement, "All people lie." I believe this to be misleading; it would be more accurate if it stated, "All people have lied."

The prophet Isaiah, in his writings of chapter 28, states to humankind, "Because ye have said, 'We have made a covenant with death, and with Hell are we at agreement.'" This statement implies that humans agree with the teaching of the lifestyle and a covenant with darkness. Liars will spend eternity in this place.

God hates pride and a lying tongue. The tongue has great power as it can speak to give life or death. The list of the types of lying above is very humorous to me since the book of Revelation says, "All liars have their place on the lake of fire," meaning all lies are death statements that smack the face of the Life-Giver. The scriptures ensure that numerous sins will secure a place in the eternal abyss where the fire is not quenched, and those sweet tiny worms never die. I find it interesting that it can be paraphrased as "all types of lies, and those who speak to them, are having an affair with Satan." Consequently, those

Ronald D. Walters

who honestly tell the truth using their lips have an honest relationship with Heaven! Truthtellers are courting the path that leads to where Jesus is forever and ever.

God hates liars because they are inappropriately affectionate with a father of lies and, by doing so, have sealed their eternal fate. However, lying is not the only death we cause with our tongues. Backbiting means speaking negatively about anyone who is not there to defend themselves. A backbiter engages openly accusatory and procreative destruction. Participating in negative verbal behavior will bring you, through the destructive power of these lies, to an eternal place far from love, joy, and peace and put you in a bed of worms in the lake of fire. It is a sobering but necessary image! We should seriously consider what we say and focus on giving life with our tongue, not causing death! You should only desire to tell the truth about Jesus and how He loves all people. Think about those things, so you can speak about those things.

One of the most truthful things we can do is repent of our sins! The vocalization of realizing that our soul was bound by darkness because of our improper actions and attitudes allows us to speak the truth that will cause Heaven to rejoice! The language of repentance is to tell God that your affair with Satan led you to break the heart of your eternal love, the groom named Jesus! Take a minute right now and repent before God and decide right now never to return to those lies. When you rise from that place of repentance, recognize that not only does Heaven rejoice, but you can also embrace people with a tongue that will speak of life!

KEY VERSES

- "But the fearful, and unbelieving, and the abominable, and murderers, and whoremongers, and sorcerers, and idolaters, and all liars, shall have their part in the lake which burneth with fire and brimstone: which is the second death" (Revelation 21:8 KJV)
- "Keep thy tongue from evil, and thy lips from speaking guile." (Psalms 34:13 KJV)

- "Lying lips are an abomination to the Lord: but they that deal truly are his delight." (Proverbs 12:22 KJV)
- "Lie not one to another, seeing that ye have put off the old man with his deeds; And have put on the new man, which is renewed in knowledge after the image of him that created him." (Colossians 3:9-10 KJV)
- "Ye are of your father the devil, and the lusts of your father ye will do. He was a murderer from the beginning and abode not in the truth because there is no truth in him. When he speaketh a lie, he speaketh of his own: for he is a liar and the father of it." (John 8:44 KJV)

Ronald D. Walters

NOTES

THE BOUNCE

EMPHASIS ON "HANDS THAT SHED INNOCENT BLOOD."

Prethought: I am not going to be a part of the shedding of innocent blood through thought or action!

Human beings kill their own species more viciously than any other mammal group. Maria Gomez and her team studied the amount of lethal violence from 1,024 different species of mammals. They found that 0.3 percent of animal deaths occur from their own species. However, with humans, that rate increases to 2.3 percent. R. Douglas Fields, Ph.D., believes this difference could partially stem from our intense desire to defend ourselves and our belongings from others outside our social group. Males are measurably more violent than females, and violence is an innate aspect of humanity.[36]

In 2008 Colin Pritchard and Tony Sayer from Bournemouth University published their survey of child homicides in England occurring over ten years. They found that children under five are most likely to be attacked by their family members. This survey highlights the difference between intra-familial and extra-familial killers. Pritchard and Sayer did not find a single case of a child under five being attacked by someone outside their family. In most cases, the assailant was the victim's parent, typically the mother, who has a mental disorder. In all the cases where the father was the assailant, they ended their own lives after their child died.[37] [32]

The Pastor's Perspective

Proverbs 6:17 asserts God hates "hands that shed innocent blood." This can be defined as human extremities that pour out the blood of innocent animals in a slaughter-like fashion and kill others within our species. The concept of innocent blood relates to being "guilt-free.," indicating there are three categories of victims: (1) young children, (2) animals that are killed only for food and sustenance, and (3) those reborn in Christ. The reborn have had an authentic, new birth experience through repentance, the remission of sins in baptism in Jesus's name, filled with the Holy Ghost, and risen to walk in the newness of life! With this definition in mind, the human species kills innocence and is a murderer.

KJV DICTIONARY DEFINITION: MURDER

MURDER, noun.

1. The act of unlawfully killing a human being with deliberate malice by a person of sound mind. To constitute murder in law, the person killing another must be of sound mind or possess his reason. The act must be done with malice. Still, malice may be implied as well as expressed.
2. An outcry when life is in danger. MUR'DER, verb.

3. To kill a human being with premeditated malice. See the Noun.
4. To destroy; to put an end to. MURDERER, noun.
5. A person in possession of his reason unlawfully kills a human being with premeditated malice.
6. Consisting in murder; done with murder; bloody; cruel; as murderous rapine.
7. Bloody; sanguinary; committing murder; as murderous tyranny.
8. Premeditating murder; as murderous intent or design.

The biblical definition of brother is "a member of your religious community," which has nothing to do with a natural bloodline but with the bloodline of Christ, as received in baptism in Jesus' name! "Agape" means love, which is defined as never between the genders, but how Christ loved us and gave His life for us. As it says in verse 15, If you see a brother with a need and do not give to that brother, you are likened to a murderer. This means that when I am not letting God's love flow through me to the members of the body of Christ, I have defined myself as a hater and a murderer. The apostle John gave a pretty high standard. If loving a brother or a sister in Christ is difficult for you, Jesus will overlook your vanity, bitterness, gossip, backbiting, lack of providing for the needs of others, and sheer willingness to let people go without because you hold the ability to flow with love. One of the most remarkable powers provided by the Holy Ghost is the ability to love my neighbor. Therefore, I can be a witness and no longer a murderer. However, the world says it is in your natural DNA that murder is acceptable and hatred is normal, We are entertained by murder; drawn to it like a mysterious magnet reaching down inside and drawing out a natural propensity to kill. Those we kill most often are the people of God who He died to redeem, and washed in the innocent blood of a Savior that successfully navigated a sinful world without sin.

Ronald D. Walters

In summary, if love is not flowing through me to the members of the body of Christ, I might as well should not plan to spend an eternity in Heaven. Without the flow of love, all that remains is the natural man, who is tribal, territorial, and easily triggered to murder those who "threaten our little paradigm". To broaden this concept; if I do not love my neighbor, I have not fully learned to love myself. I cannot see myself through the eyes of my crucified creator God. He hung on the cross to redeem my neighbor and me. It is a tragedy if I have been filled with the power of the Holy Ghost and cannot find the strength to extend love to those next to me.

Aren't you glad, Christian, that you are a lover of people? Today is your opportunity to demonstrate to Heaven that you're a vessel that He can now through because you're willing to love Him, your spouse, your children, and grandchildren. You will flow into your neighborhood with the power of light. Come on, let's grow the body of Christ by loving the unloved. I do not want to be part of those with hands that call for innocent blood to be shed and poured out for no reason!

KEY VERSE

- "For this is the message that ye heard from the beginning, that we should love one another. Not as Cain, who was of that wicked one and slew his brother. And wherefore slew him? Because his own works were evil and his brother's righteous. Marvel not, my brethren, if the world hates you. We know we have passed from death to life because we love the brethren. He that loveth not his brother abideth in death. Whosoever hateth his brother is a murderer: and ye know that no murderer hath eternal life abiding in him. Hereby perceive we the love of God because he laid down his life for us: we ought to lay down our lives for the brethren. But whoso hath this world's good, and seeth his brother have need, and shutteth up his bowels of compassion from him, how dwelleth the love of God in him? My little children, let us not love in word, neither in tongue, but in deed and truth." (John 1:1-18 KJV)

NOTES

Ronald D. Walters

EMPHASIS ON "A HEART THAT DEVISETH WICKED IMAGINATIONS" (SORROWFUL TROUBLE)

Prethought: If I let the evil imagination in
my heart, it will provoke a false start!

Sadness is an emotional response to adverse events that every person will experience occasionally. It typically does not last more than a few days and leaves after a person experiences a joyous occasion. The best treatments for sadness are expressing it and time. Depression, on the other hand, is an overwhelming sadness that has no specific reason behind it. The best treatment for depression is a combination of medication and therapy.[38]

Dr. Vikaas Sohal and his group of researchers have discovered a link between depression and anxiety and overactive communication between the two sides of the brain. When measuring the electrical activity in the brain, they found an increased activity level in the memory and emotion areas when a person is sad. This clearly shows that our moods affect on our brains. Sohal and his team found that a negative attitude occurs with increased electrical communication between the amygdala and hippocampus, which process emotions and memories, respectively. Sohal believes this is physical proof of a relationship between negative memories and emotions. We still do not know the exact relationship between memories and emotions or which part of the brain starts the chain. Still, we know a biological relationship between the two exists, which will significantly aid future research.[39]

The Pastor's Perspective

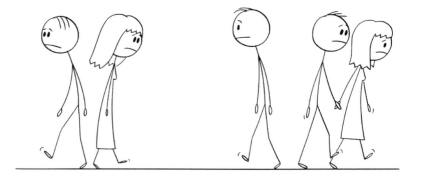

Hearts that devise "wicked" imaginations are one of the fundamental building blocks in becoming an abomination in the eyes of God. Wicked imagining involves what Solomon declares as:

KEY DEFINITIONS

- Wicked - Troubling or Sorrowful.
- Imaginations - Flights of man, evading deep thoughts of God.
- Deviseth - Continuing to make connections.

We could summarize this portion of Proverbs as one of the building blocks to becoming an abomination in continuing to have deeply troubling and sorrowful thoughts and making connections of those thoughts to the people around us.

Why would God hate this sort of thinking? Why would perpetual sadness and its connection to human beings put us in jeopardy of losing out on God?

KEY VERSES

- "And the Lord...he will be with thee, he will not fail thee, neither forsake thee: fear not, neither be dismayed." (Deuteronomy 31:8 KJV)
- "The righteous cry and the Lord heareth, and delivereth them out of all their troubles. The Lord is nigh unto them that are of a broken heart; and saveth such as be of a contrite spirit." (Psalm 34:17-18 KJV)
- "Blessed are they that mourn: for they shall be comforted." (Matthew 5:4 KJV)
- "Casting all your care upon him; for he careth for you." (1 Peter 5:7 KJV)
- "For his anger endureth but a moment; in his favor is life: weeping may endure for a night, but joy cometh in the morning." (Psalm 30:5 KJV)

Christians must realize when they meet Jesus that they are "born again." God, as the creator, understands that life brings sorrow and pain. However, we become "a new creature when we meet Him. The Lord says, within the context of being a new creature, "All things have become new." All things mean everything, including our hearts, souls, minds, and physical strengths. Suppose I allow my heart to continue connecting negative emotions in historical opinions to current people. In that case, I judge them by my historical paradigm. Therefore, I am continuing in my sadness, which means I have no joy or strength. The power of God does not create frail, sad, angry, or bitter people. It makes new creatures who walk with joy and peace and have found happiness!

The experience of the new birth is all-encompassing. When we follow His instructions and "meditate on the Lord, day and night," we will delight in serving God through submission and love. We are just human beings meandering through the sorrow of life, continually reminded of how people have failed us and how sad we are to be alive.

The Bible says, "What fellowship does Christ have with an unbeliever." This verse indicates that we will not be the same as unbelievers once we become Christian. When we follow the Lord through His Word, the darkness that once made us sad and the memories of personal pain and loss can no longer move through us to affect those around us. Being perpetually unhappy after meeting Jesus is a step toward becoming an abomination. It robs the Lord of the opportunity for us to love our neighbors since our hearts connect sadness to the people around us.

Sadness robs us of evangelistic zeal and the desire to introduce others to Jesus, who corrected all our sadness! If the Jesus I serve was not strong enough to give me happiness in today's experiences, why would I ever introduce anyone else to Him? It is like a person who has faith but no works, who will continue to walk in the lust of the eyes, the lust of the flesh, and the pride of life. Therefore, they will never be able to have those good and happy thoughts or feelings since they have not connected the activity to their beliefs. These believers will remain sad, unusable, and even dangerous to the people closest to them.

The Lord does not hate you if you are a person who struggles with a dour outlook, continually judging others because you don't feel good about yourself, but He does hate that pathology! When He said, "Come out from among them and be separate saith the Lord," He wants us to include the verse, "We should come away from our own thoughts and let this mind be in you which was also in Christ Jesus." It would be terrible to go through life sad, then to be sent away from God because we were ineffective witnesses.

Will you let Him now wipe away your tears and let the word of God heal your sorrow? Meditate on that question today instead of the memories that hurt so deeply. Begin to have a new thought process about life as you see sinners through your own eyes of forgiveness and your ability to carry a cross. This start will make a difference. Let the joy of the Lord fill your heart so you may become what He has called you to be! Remember, you are awesome in the eyes of God!

NOTES

Ronald D. Walters

DAY 23: HATRED LESSON 6

EMPHASIS ON "FEET THAT BE SWIFT IN THE RUNNING TO MISCHIEF."

Prethought: I need to run to the good
life and avoid falling into strife!

reed has existed in humanity since the beginning. When used well, it is the driving force behind progress. However, greed can also cause economic misery in a culture run by materialism. There are seven main warning signs of greed in a person. The first is being self-centered with no regard for others. The second is having intense envy for what others have, and the third is not caring how their actions affect others' feelings. The fourth is wanting more than what they have; fifth, they easily manipulate others to their will. Sixth, they want immediate results of their greed. Seventh, they have no regard for morals and ethics in cheating their way to their goal. The hard part for those affected by someone else's greed is waiting for them to change.

The greedy person must notice their faults and desire to change for themselves. This can be difficult because greed affects their view of themselves and others. It is our job to guide them once they need it.[40]

The Pastor's Perspective

Feet that are swift and running to mischief! In Strong's dictionary, this phrase means that the sole of the foot is set in the greediest direction to scatter and idolatrize the destruction of pastureland while murdering others and emphasizing lustful self-satisfaction. Whew, it sounds like everybody else. Not me, right? It would be great if I could stop now and not be defined or break down the terrible, consequential choice to mindlessly follow the culture we live in now.

KEY VERSE

- "And Saul was consenting unto his death. Moreover, at that time, there was a great persecution against the church which was at Jerusalem; and they were all scattered abroad throughout the regions of Judaea and Samaria, except the apostles. And devout men carried Stephen to his burial and made great lamentation over him. As for Saul, he made havoc on the church, entering into every house and haling men and women committed them to prison." (Acts 8:1- 3 KJV)

Through the persecution of Jesus Christ by the Jews, the Church at Jerusalem was born. Political leaders and religious leaders not only plotted but consented and advocated for the death of the one truly innocent man who ever lived, Jesus Christ. They quickly, and under the cloak of night, judged, pummeled, beat, and led Him away to be crucified. That was when we chose to crucify innocence, unconditional love, and the One who had concern only for others and not for Himself.

Ronald D. Walters

The cross demonstrates the utter and complete yielding of the sole of humanity's feet, growling and without compunction, murdering and celebrating the death of deliverance from evil, hope for humanity, and the greatest love we would ever see demonstrated...we crucified him.

We learn about the church's birth in Acts, Chapter 2 first coming to the lost children of Israel with the great Apostle Peter's preaching. The Apostle Peter delivers the message that corrects our behavior...repent. In Acts chapter 8, just before the birth of what will be the Gentile church as recorded in Acts chapter 10, we see present the Apostle Peter. Peter was the one on the day of the crucifixion who did not consent to the death of the innocent Christ. But in in this scenario of Acts chapter 8, there is a greedy crowd that have the soles of their feet set to pursue the death of the innocent Stephen. Present also was Saul of Tarsus who would become the great Apostle Paul to whom it is recorded that he was "consenting to the death of Stephen." Shortly after this murder and death of Stephen in Acts chapter 10, God moves through the birth of the church of Jesus Christ beyond the children of Israel and into the backyard of my humanity...The Gentiles.

This brings us to the concept in Proverbs chapter 6 that you and I, as gentiles, must overcome the propensity to swiftly, greedily run toward the idea that "I am saved, and others are lost." Then, I consent to the culture of death to murder my neighbor, fellow workers, or others while I religiously sit in the safety of His love and refuse to love others. I'm greedy for my salvation but deny it to those around me. They could also be innocent of His death if they would repent. I don't want to be trapped by Satan. To have only the great motivation to see myself saved while becoming greedy as I consent by religiously judgmental silence to the rest of the world being sent to a dark place. Motivation, complete loss, and the pursuit of murder are not only about taking pleasure in others' being destroyed, but means I am greedy in the search for my own loss as I consent to the murder of this group of beautiful, hopeful people. These are people bound by sin.

The choice to be a sinner comes naturally to the human species. Nevertheless, let's not be like the unconverted Saul of Tarsus. Saul, before being reborn, was determined to destroy the body of Christ through religious judgment. Saul consented to the death of innocents, such as Stephen, who was stoned (Acts 7:54-59). Jesus provided the greatest opportunity to self-judge when He said, "Let him without sin cast the first stone." Christians can become so trapped in greed and desire to be saved that the soles of their feet are motivated by a lust for salvation. We consent to our neighbor's death through silence when we are greedy. But as Romans 1:32 says, "Who knowing the judgment of God, that they which commit such things are worthy of death, not only do the same but have pleasure in them that do them." People who have accepted Jesus know better but choose not to be better. Therefore, they decide to live in a culture of death, darkness, and the pursuit of lust and so they stay lost in sin.

I am glad I am not like the others lost in sin. Remember what we have studied this day and consider this verse as we keep our walk with God.

KEY VERSE

- "And he spake this parable unto certain which trusted in themselves that they were righteous, and despised others: Two men went up into the temple to pray; the one a Pharisee, and the other a publican. The Pharisee stood and prayed thus with himself. God, I thank thee that I am not as other men are, extortioners, unjust, adulterers, or even as this publican. I fast twice a week, and I give tithes of all that I possess. And the publican, standing afar off, would not lift up so much as his eyes unto Heaven, but smote upon his breast, saying, God be merciful to me a sinner. I tell you; this man went down to his house justified rather than the other: for every one that exalteth himself shall be abased, and he that humbleth himself shall be exalted." (Luke 18:9-14 KJV)

NOTES

Ronald D. Walters

THE BOUNCE

EMPHASIS ON "A FALSE WITNESS THAT SPEAKETH LIES."

Prethought: Focus on the witness of truth
so the lie will never apply to you!

False accusations are untrue claims of wrongdoing. There are three main types of false accusations. The first is an entirely false allegation. The second is an assertion allegation which accurately describes events, but of which the accused person is innocent. The third type is an allegation which mixes together false and true descriptions of events. False accusations can be either intentional or accidental for any number of reasons.[41]

People often form intense opinions about others with a single piece of information. When those opinions are negative, it can lead to false accusations. Defending oneself against false accusations can be likened to torture due to emotional and mental strain on the person. Freud believed this internal emotional pain was the worst human experience.[42] [37]

The Pastor's Perspective

Read Proverbs 6:19. A false witness refers to an injurious falsehood spoken in a court of law with exuberance and excitable passion, a human pretentious false prophecy! Before moving to the list of verses for today's study, please take a moment to read Jesus's words in Matthew chapter 7:1, "Judge not!" Now, take a moment to consider these other verses:

These three witnesses of how our God looks at false information include the law of Moses, Solomon's wisdom, and God's words manifest in the flesh. We should take note of this concept and determine that we will not be guilty of this. When considering the psychology of accusation, we have to note another person's perception and what motivates their actions. However, no other individual can be solely determined by our judgment or know precisely what caused a person to act in any particular way. The judgmental Christian is guilty of assuming what the word of God leaves in its own authority or God's destined role of His child. A judgmental Christian is guilty of assuming the role of what the Word of God leaves in its own authority: "Dividing asunder

between soul and spirit and as a discerner of the thoughts and the intentions of the heart" (Hebrews 4:12). The nature of false accusation belongs only to the judge and is punishable by eternity away from God. For that reason, Moses said not to do it, Solomon said God hates it, and Jesus said, "In the same way you judge others, you will be judged" (Matthew 7:2)!

Two instances in Proverbs 6 display building blocks to becoming an abomination before God related to lying. The first one is that God hates a lying tongue.

Ronald D. Walters

The second one says God hates "a false witness that speaketh lies." The first reference is accurately paraphrased, noting that anyone who lies is in jeopardy of being hated by God, much like Esau (Malachi 1:3). The second instance relates to the "court of law" by using the word "witness." This would indicate that instead of lying about stuff you've been doing, you are trying to publicly accuse someone of being permanently guilty vehemently and with great passion.

Being judgmental is like calling someone who gives you an angry look "a hater" or someone who looks at another person with improper sexual motivations a cheater or adulterer. Although the haters and the adulterers are to face eternal punishment, the word of God says those on the accusation side, or the judgment side, will also face separation from God. Does that seem unfair? It makes sense when you look at how the Lord Jehovah God wants us to live a full life of peace and happiness. When I waste mental energy engaging in negative thought processes, accusing or judging others (even those I believe are guilty), I rob myself of the three tenets of Christian living: love, joy, and peace.

We can be so consumed, mentally, by the wrongs of others that we become a victim of our own rampaging wrath. A Christian might never voice condemnation, but holding onto resentment and pridefully looking down on someone for real or assumed mistakes is wrong. As Christians, we are called to be peaceful, loving, and engaging with others in a bond of peace. Let the cross and the beautiful Savior hung on it judge what others intended to do or actually did. Let us think well of all people and live fully with joy and enthusiasm so that we can lead others to the cross. Do not view others as unforgiven sinners; see them as pre-forgiven individuals who will see what the power of forgiveness and repentance offers them and others. It sounds like a joyful way to live, the way God intended for us to live!

- "Thou shalt not bear false witness against thy neighbor." (Exodus 20:16 KJV)
  - o "Thou shalt not bear false witness" forbids: Speaking falsely in any matter, lying, equivocating, and in any way devising and designing to deceive our neighbor. Alternatively, speaking unjustly against our neighbor, to the prejudice of his reputation.
- "These six things doth the Lord hate: yea, seven are an abomination unto him: A proud look, a lying tongue, and hands that shed innocent blood. A heart that deviseth wicked imaginations, feet that be swift in the running to mischief, A false witness that speaketh lies, and he that soweth discord among brethren." (Proverbs 6:16-19 KJV)
- "A false witness shall not be unpunished, and he that speaketh lies shall not escape." (Proverbs 19:5 KJV)
- "A false witness shall not be unpunished, and he that speaketh lies shall perish." (Proverbs 19:9 KJV)
- "Wherefore putting away lying, speak every man truth with his neighbor: for we are members one of another." (Ephesians 4:25 KJV)
- "But the fearful, and unbelieving, and the abominable, and murderers, and whoremongers, and sorcerers, and idolaters, and all liars, shall have their part in the lake which burneth with fire and brimstone: which is the second death." (Revelation 21:8 KJV)

NOTES

THE BOUNCE

DAY 25: HATRED LESSON 8

EMPHASIS ON "HE THAT SOWETH DISCORD AMONG BRETHREN."

Prethought: Helping people get along
is a beautiful love song!

People with high-conflict personalities tend to blame others for their problems because they are unwilling or unable to realize they are the cause. People with high-conflict personalities have four essential traits: consistent targets of their blame, all-or-nothing thinking, unmanaged emotions, and extreme behaviors. They may

also have characteristics indicative of five different personality disorders. The first disorder is antisocial disorder. These are not people who "just don't feel like hanging out," but they combine charm with cruelty to reach their goals. The second disorder is narcissistic personality disorder. These people have fragile and inflated self-esteem while constantly putting down those "below" them. The third disorder is a borderline

Ronald D. Walters

personality disorder. These people cling to those close to them and lash out at slight or perceived abandonment. The fourth disorder is paranoid personality disorder. These people are very suspicious of those around them because they believe others are only there to attack them. The last disorder is a histrionic personality disorder. These people seek constant attention and tend to cause drama with their exaggerated stories. However, not every person with these disorders has a high-conflict personality. If they do not have consistent targets for their blame, they do not have a high-conflict personality.[43]

The Pastor's Perspective

The church's inception is recorded in Acts chapter 2 as happening later: "They were all in one place and in one accord," indicating everybody was getting along and everyone had pulled together to form an alliance. That alliance was then blessed by God's new and dynamic presence in the church. Suddenly, there came a sound from Heaven when the people got along. The Lord of glory poured out His Spirit immediately and ushered in what is now "the church age." This church age will end with something called "the rapture." This is an excellent catching away of what He defines as "the body of Christ" or "the bride without spot or wrinkle!" If you pursue the scripture further, it says that God adds to the church when the body of Christ has favor with God and with man. Assuming we can all learn to get along, we can all be prepared to go up in His heavenly presence. Sometimes, people with high conflict personality disorders refuse to rein in every thought to the obedience of Christ. They verbally spew all the toxins put into their thinking through childhood trauma and improper examples they have witnessed.

The danger of allowing your high-conflict personality disorder to manifest within the group of people whom the Lord has redeemed is that God hates it. "Well, you don't understand, Pastor; I just don't always feel good about people." God hates it because He loves the people our words divide us from. Other excuses are, "I'm just a gossip," "They were looking at me funny," or, "When I am troubled by something, I just have to talk with someone about it." God hates it!

Those are examples of the six things the Lord hates and seven that are an abomination unto Him. We ruin our reputation because we perceive some falsehood. We destroy our personal relationships by blaming others for our terrible self-esteem because we refuse to learn, behave, or trust others. In John 3, Jesus indicated that to be a part of the bride of Christ and be pulled from this world when He returns we must "be born again of water and spirit." Being reborn gives us a brand-new Father, God, and hope that we can accept others. Therefore, why allow these building blocks to be an abomination unto God?

This is the most troubling to a Pastor. This is where the group can grow, but because of one personality disorder, many can also be hurt. Stop allowing yourself to think improperly about other people. Remember the key verse from Matthew 7. Judging others will be the gateway to eternal separation from God. Thus, when you enter the church, check your high-conflict personality at the door and desire to love unconditionally! Before walking in, accept that you must stop judging everybody according to the disorder of your thoughts.

KEY VERSES

- "For lack of wood the fire goes out, and where there is no whisperer, contention quiets down." (Proverbs 26:20 NASB)
- "For you are still fleshly. For since there is jealousy and strife among you, are you not fleshly, and are you not walking like mere men?" (1 Corinthians 3:3 NASB)

- "Therefore, the Jews were grumbling about Him because He said, "I am the bread that came down out of heaven." (John 6:41-43 NASB)
- They said, "Is not this Jesus, the son of Joseph, whose father and mother we know? How does He now say, 'I have come down out of heaven'?" Jesus answered and said to them, "Do not grumble among yourselves." (John 6:34 NASB)
- "Now I urge you, brethren, keep your eye on those who cause dissensions and hindrances contrary to the teaching which you learned, and turn away from them." (Romans 16:17 NASB)
- "Remind them of these things, and solemnly charge them in the presence of God not to wrangle about words, which is useless and leads to the ruin of the hearers." (2 Timothy 2:14 NASB)

- "As I urged you upon my departure for Macedonia, remain on at Ephesus so that you may instruct certain men not to teach strange doctrines, nor to pay attention to myths and endless genealogies, which give rise to mere speculation rather than furthering the administration of God which is by faith." (1 Timothy 1:3-4 NASB)
- "Keeping away from strife is an honor for a man, but any fool will quarrel." (Proverbs 20:3 NASB)
- "Make friends quickly with your opponent at law while you are with him on the way so that your opponent may not hand you over to the judge, and the judge to the officer, and you be thrown into prison." (Matthew 5:25 NASB)

NOTES

Ronald D. Walters

PART V

....

WORDS

THE BOUNCE

COMMUNICATING VERBALLY

Prethought: The words I use are tools.
Speaking wrongly would make me a fool!

Time Magazine published an article describing an experiment by Rev. Franklin Loehr, a chemist trained at Illinois Monmouth college and Presbyterian minister, who tested two rows of seeds planted from the same package. All received the same amount of watering and care, but one row was cursed by a woman, and the other row was prayed for. The results of this experiment were shocking. One hundred percent of the seeds prayed for flourished and bore fruit, but the cursed ones became twisted and distorted with no fruit evident, and they died. The research team looked to Mark 11:20, where Christ cursed a fig tree, and in a matter of hours, it was "dried up from the roots."[44]

The Pastor's Perspective

The continuous fight science has with Christianity and God's Word is an immense struggle for what is called faith. The scriptures declare, "the tongue has the power of life or death" (Proverbs 18:21 NIV). The experiment above provides a great picture of this truth being enacted by a scientist. The proof of the death grip of words is much more prevalent in our culture.

How many homes have been destroyed by death, divorce, hate, accusations of infidelity, or what Solomon referred to as a wife's contentious words? How many single people don't self-speak love, acceptance, and the power to grow? Countless children have been victimized by harsh parental communication demeaning their intelligence and value! Take control of your life today by taking control of your words! Let the root, seed, and fruit of who you are in Christ be evidence to the world of all that is good and lovely!

Your life as an individual human being has the seed power to become a mighty nation or a light in a darkened world. If you're married, think of your marriage as a seed planted in the ground. The fruit of our marriage is like the sampling study of the scientist referenced above! If we let the seeds receive negative words and cursing, we will have the fruit of that. Love can and does die every day; that is why the Lord our God said, "Man cannot live by bread only but by every word which proceeds out of the mouth of God" (Luke 4:4).

I want to let my words give life today, so when I wake up in the morning, I greet the Lord with a hearty welcome into my life. I next speak words of encouragement to myself as a husband and father. I will speak to my wife words of love and affirmation and to my children words of hope and life. To those I am fortunate enough to mentor, I will speak words of hope and courage in a culture trying to make us fear and isolate ourselves!

 Come on, Christian, and speak enormous words of love and life today, and watch a "newness" come into your circle of love! Be the power of blessing and stop the flow of cursing. This is the most extraordinary power we will ever know! I am on your side.

Ronald D. Walters

NOTES

THE

BOUNCE

STOP NEGATIVE COMMUNICATION

Prethought: I choose to speak life and
reduce my personal strife!

The Trump administration did not allow the CDC to use seven specific words when making budget fund proposals: evidence-based, science-based, vulnerable, fetus, transgender, diversity, or entitlement. When this was announced by The Washington Post, the public health and policy communities were in an uproar. Oregon Democratic Senator Jeff Merkley tweeted, 'Are you kidding me?!?!' The American Public Health Association wrote, 'This. Is. Unacceptable.' Does it matter if a particular language is avoided in official documents sent to government agencies? Scientific American interviewed Lera Boroditsky, a cognitive scientist, about what happens when we use certain words and not others in our daily life or work? According to Boroditsky, words have power. Saying that a hamburger is 80 percent lean or 20 percent fat communicates the same. However, people perceive the 80 percent lean hamburger as healthier than the 20 percent fat hamburger. You can choose how others think about something by framing and discussing it.[45]

The Pastor's Perspective

Here, the lesson is to stop letting words that kill out of our mouths. Why would I continue to speak poorly toward others when God's Word and scientific data suggest that words have power?

SOLOMON

- "A man's belly shall be satisfied with the fruit of his mouth; with the increase of his lips shall he be filled. Death and life are in the power of the tongue: and they that love it shall eat the fruit thereof. Whoso findeth a wife findeth a good thing and obtaineth favor of the LORD. The poor useth entreaties, but the rich answereth roughly. A man that hath friends must shew himself friendly: and there is a friend that sticketh closer than a brother." (Proverbs 18:20-24 KJV)
- Principle- Words determine direction.

ISAIAH

- "I have seen his ways and will heal him: I will lead him and restore comforts unto him and his mourners. I create the fruit of the lips; peace to him that is far off, and to him that is near, saith the Lord, and I will heal him. But the wicked are like the troubled sea, when it cannot rest, whose waters cast up mire and dirt. There is no peace...to the wicked." (Isaiah 57:18-21 KJV)
- Principle- What you speak, He creates.

THE APOSTLE PETER

- "Likewise, ye wives, be in subjection to your own husbands; that, if any obey not the word, they also may without the word be won by the conversation of the wives; While they behold your chaste conversation coupled with fear. Whose adorning let it not be that outward adorning of plaiting the hair, and of wearing of gold, or of putting on of apparel; But let it be the hidden man of the heart, in that which is not corruptible, even the ornament of a meek and quiet spirit, which is in the sight of God of great price." (1 Peter 3:1-4 KJV)

- Principle- The female gender has word authority in relationships. This pertains not only to marriage but also to who we are as a bride of Christ. We influence Heaven through the words we use on earth. Peter says to wives, your words within the context of your marital relationship are more potent in your husband's hearing than the words that proceed out of the mouth of God.

The belief that we have the right to speak about people, institutions, leadership, or church culture however we 'feel' speaks to our ignorance as humans and clears a path to spend eternity without God. The politicians of the day react harshly when threatened with the loss of specific terms from their shared vocabulary. They realize that if you replace particular terms, you correct the misappropriated thought. They absolutely recognize the scientific fact that you shape opinion with your words.

 What would happen within the body of Christ if we took heed to how we talk to other people and about other people regarding the exceptional individuals that make up the 'church'? A brother to a brother? A sister to a sister? A parent to child? A husband to a wife? A wife to a husband? A teacher to students? Students to their teachers?

Perhaps, if we are lonely, we could recognize that we likely have no friends because our language is death. Our marriage is dissatisfying because our language is death. Our finances struggle because our language is death. We are not content with who He created us to be because we speak death. Take advantage of your social standing to lock yourself in with a positive mind. Think well, begin to speak well, and start to live well. People judge you by the words you use, but the Word of God indicates we judge ourselves by the words we use.

Ronald D. Walters

I have said many times, friend, that you are exactly where you thought you would be now. As we have studied this concept, we see that your life reflects the words you alone have used. He has definitely created the fruit of your lips. Be glad that our God never fails to give us life or death according to our words.

NOTES

Ronald D. Walters

CHOOSE WORDS CAREFULLY

Prethought: I will never regret the things I do not say so happy words make for a happy day!

The words you choose become a reality because reality is subjective. This truth causes problems when your mind is consistently negative. However, you can change this by using positive self-talk to reshape how you see your situations. This "top-down" processing is how the various parts of your brain work together. Your prefrontal cortex is the "up brain," while your subconscious is the "down brain." The prefrontal cortex sends directions and messages to the subconscious, forming and storing memories. Making your brain think only positive self-talk can make you see the world more optimistically. Psychologist Gary Lupyan says, "Perceptual systems do the best with inherently ambiguous inputs by putting them in the context of what we know and expect. Studies like this are helping us show that language is a powerful tool for shaping perceptual systems, acting as a top-down signal to perceptual processes. In the case of vision, what we consciously perceive is deeply shaped by our knowledge and expectations. A simple "yes" or "no" can also significantly influence our perceptions. Thinking "yes" can tell our brain to go ahead, while thinking "no" can tell our brain to stop. Mary Kay said, "If you think you can, you can. If you think you can't, you're right."[46]

The Pastor's Perspective

The above-referenced article really demonstrates well that the truth written in the word of God concerning faith (confidence) is played out in everyday life by those who do not profess to know Christ.

When the psychological community outside of God confirms what the word of God has boldly declared for thousands of years, it stands to reason that we would listen and do what these two declare.

Therefore, speak something positive to yourself, someone close to you, or someone you want to draw near you again. Words can bring healing or inflame anger. The choice is all up to you.

Incredibly, the entire journey of the human experience begins with the words "In the beginning, God created the heavens and the earth" (Genesis 1:1 KJV). It says further that "God said let there be" is the tool of His creation (Genesis KJV). So we should use our words to let positive things begin for us. Let there be positive words in your life today by using good words with the good people around you. Go get them, Christian!

KEY VERSES

- "Faith is the substance of things hoped for, the evidence of things not seen. For by it, the elders obtained a good report. Through faith, we understand that the world was framed by the word of God. Things that are seen are not made of things that do appear. By faith, Abel offered God a more excellent sacrifice

Ronald D. Walters

than Cain, by which he obtained witness that he was righteous, God testifying of his gifts: and by it, he being dead yet speaketh. By faith, Enoch was translated that he should not see death; and was not found because God had translated him: for before his translation, he had this testimony that he pleased God. But without faith, it is impossible to please him: for he that cometh to God must believe that he is and that he is a rewarder of them that diligently seek him." (Hebrews 11:1-6 KJV)

- "Be careful for nothing, but in every thing by prayer and supplication with thanksgiving let your requests be made known unto God. And the peace of God, which passeth all understanding, shall keep your hearts and minds through Christ Jesus. Finally, brethren, whatsoever things are true, whatsoever things are honest, whatsoever things are just, whatsoever things are pure, whatsoever things are lovely, whatsoever things are of good report; if there be any virtue, and if there be any praise, think on these things. Those things, which ye have both learned, and received, and heard, and seen in me, do: and the God of peace shall be with you." (Philippians 4:6-9 KJV)

- "Let the words of my mouth, and the meditation of my heart, be acceptable in thy sight, O LORD, my strength, and my redeemer." (Psalms 19:14 KJV)

NOTES

Ronald D. Walters

THE BOUNCE

GROUP TALK

Prethought: The words I say have power so I will focus to be positive...hour by hour!

Ana Paula Frezatto Martins, a physical education teacher in Brazil, arranged her class in a circle around two cups of sealed grains. To one cup, the students were asked to say negative things such as, "You are useless" and "You can't accomplish anything." To the second glass, the kids were asked to say positive things such as, "You are special," "You can accomplish anything," and "You are smart." Martins then put the rice cups aside, and when the kids checked on them later, the rice in the "love cup" had fermented, while the rice in the "hate cup" had become dark and moldy. This experiment led many students to be more positive in their daily lives.

Ten-year-old Anita Santini Trevisan said, "When you say something nice, like 'You can do it,' you feel that in your heart." Henrique Kloster noted, "The damage of negativity is bigger than we can imagine. There are two ways to say things. The right way is to praise the good side of others with the eyes of the heart, not the eyes we see." Masaru Emoto was the originator of this rice experiment. He also performed a similar experiment testing distilled and natural water frozen into crystals and exposed to different human emotions. Emoto wrote, "In all of these experiments... we always observed beautiful crystals after giving good words, playing good music, and showing, playing, or offering prayer to water. On the other hand, we observed disfigured crystals in the opposite situation."[47]

The Pastor's Perspective

The concept is really quite simple. Your heart is deceitful and desperately wicked; left to its own devices, it will think there are clouds and rain even when the sky is blue and sunny. The "misconception of intent" can bring us to a place where we use words like daggers. We use them to stab the people we have pledged to love and support with our vows in a marriage, through giving birth to children, to those who are our neighbors, or by God's will against fellow church members.

The repeated rice in a jar experiment has proven that words and the intention of the human heart projected through those words have the power to destroy living matter! If words have that kind of authority and nature, consider what you have done to those you are responsible for loving through the eyes of God.

Some of you say, "It is the other person's fault that I am angry, frustrated, or using these words." The reality is that nothing stays in your heart unless you allow it to, and you shall be judged for everything that escapes your lips. I say to all of us: before we go one word further, repent! To clarify, stop speaking before you say another word of destructive intent. Right now, where you are, repent of your words at this moment of revelation! Repentance is not for the other person to feel good, but you can feel whole! Repentance tells God you are sorry for murdering love, destroying people, and derailing those closest to you. Again, repent before saying one more word; make peace with God in Jesus' name.

Ronald D. Walters

To those of you who need no repentance because your words have been fitly spoken, and you who have a disciplined tongue: take a moment now to commit that you will continue to say only life-giving words to those closest to you.

 Come on, Christian, you've got this. We can repent and redirect our words while we're still breathing. Our terms matter when we thoughtfully consider our eternal destination. Speak life.

KEY VERSES

- "A hypocrite with his mouth destroyeth his neighbor: but through knowledge shall the just be delivered." (Proverbs 11:9 KJV)
- "A good man out of the good treasure of his heart bringeth forth that which is good; and an evil man out of the evil treasure of his heart bringeth forth that which is evil: for of the abundance of the heart his mouth speaketh." (Luke 6:45 KJV)
- "He that keepeth his mouth keepeth his life: but he that openeth wide his lips shall have destruction." (Prov 13:3 KJV)
- "A wholesome tongue is a tree of life: but perverseness therein is a breach in the spirit." (Prov 15:4 KJV)
- "Therefore whatsoever ye have spoken in darkness shall be heard in the light, and that which ye have spoken in the ear in closets shall be proclaimed upon the housetops." (Luke 12:3 KJV)
- "But I say unto you, that every idle word that men shall speak, they shall give account thereof in the day of judgment." (Matthew 12:36 KJV)

NOTES

Ronald D. Walters

THE BOUNCE

WORDS REHEARSED MAKE THINGS BETTER... OR WORSE

Prethougth: The words spoken into the air will show that I hate or I care!

Ikea demonstrated the power of words by using two of their plants for a social experiment to raise awareness of the effects of bullying. For 30 days, two plants were placed in a school and subjected to two identical environments. The only difference was that one plant was situated near recordings of positive words, and the other was bombarded by negative comments. After 30 days, the "bullied" plant started wilting, while the complimented plant flourished!

If you were put into an fMRI scanner, an imaging system that can record the brain's neural changes, and saw the word "NO" on the screen faster than you could even realize, your brain would release dozens of stress-producing hormones. These chemicals interrupt the processes in your brain, which impairs logic, reason, language processing, and communication. Simply glancing at a list of negative words can make an anxious or depressed person feel worse. The more you play them over in your brain, the more you can damage the structures that regulate your memory, feelings, and emotions. This will disrupt your sleep, appetite, and even your ability to experience happiness.

When talking to others, if you verbalize negativity or even slightly frown, more stress chemicals are released in your and the listener's brains. They will then have higher anxiety and be more irritable, making it harder to cooperate and trust. Even gathering with people of a negative mindset can increase prejudices in your mind. Any form of negative thinking will release destructive chemicals into your brain, and this is especially true with children. The more negative words they hear, the more likely they will be highly anxious and stressed later in life. However, if you lead in positivity, your children will show a much more productive life.

Negative thinking is also self-fulfilling. The more negative thought space you use in your mind, the harder it is to stop. However, the damage is far worse when those thoughts are verbalized through anger. Anger sends alarm messages through an angry person's brain that interfere with the decision-making frontal lobe, increasing the likelihood of acting irrationally. Words like poverty, illness, death, and divorce provoke fear, which stimulates specific chemicals in the brain that have an overall negative impact. Even if these thoughts are fantasies, the thalamus (sends sensory information) and the amygdala (deals with emotions) react as though the ideas were real. This makes it seem like the human brain is designed to worry, but we can take steps to prevent a negative spiral by stopping and asking ourselves if this threat is real or perceived. If it's not real, you have just interrupted the amygdala's reaction, which then reduces the likelihood that your memory will retain the negativity.[48]

Ronald D. Walters

The Pastor's Perspective

KEY VERSES

- "Keep back thy servant also from presumptuous sins; let them not have dominion over me: then shall I be upright, and I shall be innocent from the great transgression. Let the words of my mouth and the meditation of my heart be acceptable in thy sight, O Lord, my strength, and my redeemer." (Psalm 19:13-14 KJV)

KEY DEFINITION

- Pre·sump·tu·ous (adjective) - (of a person or their behavior) failing to observe the limits of what is permitted or appropriate.

The experiments mentioned above demonstrate that members of secular society are discovering what the word of God has directed us to for millennia. Many people who claim to be Christian for many years believe they have some dispensation that allows them to operate outside the Commandments or the guidelines in God's Word. We treat each other poorly, think negatively about others, and gossip about things we don't understand. We have no right to share our opinions. We destructively move through relationships, leaving a trail of brokenness, despair, and bad feelings behind us. All because we presume that we are okay.

In Psalm 19, David indicates that a person pursuing the God of the Bible should be concerned about being presumptuous. The only way to be saved from the sin of presuming we're above the law or have a right to demonstrate negativity is to check our attitude at the door and begin to be "acceptable in thy sight, O Lord," with the thoughts we think and the words we say (Psalm 19:14).

In the previous study, we read about how humans will be judged for every idle word. However, we continue to spew venom, darkness, and anxiety-laden terms out of our mouths toward the children of the Lord, such as ourselves, spouses, children, and others. I don't want to be offensive, but shame on the husband who speaks or thinks negatively about his wife. Shame on a wife who believes she has a right to tear down her husband in private or, what would be considered worse by God, tear down a father in the presence of his children. Shame on any young person who uses destructive words or allows gossip magazines to be your meditation.

The real issue is that we don't value the things that took Him to the cross. The people, the relationships that they have with themselves and their neighbors. I have committed a presumptuous sin if I tear into another human being with my negative thoughts or words. I caused the person who was the target of my words to be less than adequate at loving themselves and, thus, less effective in loving their neighbor. Am I irrational to think I can tear people down and the Lord will build me up? Like Toby Mac says, "Speak life … speak hope, speak love."[49]

Today, you can think you are happy, speak yourself into joy, or choose not to think yourself happy. However, the excuses come out: "You don't understand how hard it is," "The history of my life tells me that I should be negative," "I've had a callous life," etc. Can you imagine eternity separated from the Lord if you think life is tough? This thought should cause you to truly repent of those things that have happened to you and through you. Begin right now to speak positively. My friend Charles Robinson once said, "Eternity is a long time to be wrong." Come on, Christian, don't just think about it; act on it. Speak something positive before you take one more step in your life! Before you take one more breath. Even if it is just into the air toward God, think a positive thought and speak a positive word. Repent or perish is the way that Jesus put it. Even though we won't know who is missing, Heaven will be lonely without you (for you).

Ronald D. Walters

I leave you with this last thought: why do we say "I do" to relationships, friendships, and even experiences with God, Then, then spend the rest of our time tearing people down and destroying what He is trying to build? I recommend we change, and we change now! Take a minute and say something good now, think something good now, and reach out to the people around you with good words. Don't hesitate, do it now! Literally, stop what you're doing. Now, text a positive message, speak a positive word and begin on the first step to a brand new you.

NOTES

Ronald D. Walters

BIBLIOGRAPHY

1   Reference
2   Carter, Sherrie Bourg. "Emotions Are Contagious-Choose Your Company Wisely." Psychology Today, Sussex Publishers, 20 Oct. 2012, https://www.psychologytoday.com/us/blog/high-octane-women/201210/emotions-are-contagious-choose-your-company-wisely
3   "Anger." Psychology Today, Sussex Publishers, https://www.psychologytoday.com/us/basics/anger
4   "What Is Cognition & Cognitive Behaviour." Cambridge Cognition, 19 Aug. 2015, https://www.cambridgecognition.com/blog/entry/what-is-cognition#:~:text=Cognition%20is%20defined%20as%20%27the,used%20to%20guide%20your%20behavior.
5   "Panic Disorder & Panic Attacks; Symptoms, Causes, Treatment." Cleveland Clinic, 2018, Panic Attacks: Panic Disorder, Anxiety Disorder, Symptoms, Causes (clevelandclinic.org)
6   "Anxiety Disorders: Types, Causes, Symptoms & Treatments." Cleveland Clinic, 2017, https://my.clevelandclinic.org/health/diseases/9536-anxiety-disorders
7   Lancer, Darlene. "Do You Trust Too Much or Too Little?" Psychology Today, Sussex Publishers, 11 Dec. 2019, www.psychologytoday.com/us/blog/toxic-relationships/201912/do-you-trust-too-much-or-too-little
8   Fields, R. Douglas. "Humans Are Genetically Predisposed to Kill Each Other." Psychology Today, Sussex Publishers, 2 Oct. 2016, https://www.psychologytoday.com/us/blog/the-new-brain/201610/humans-are-genetically-predisposed-kill-each-other
9   Firestone, Lisa. "The Value of Sadness." Psychology Today, Sussex Publishers, 30 Jul. 2015. https://www.psychologytoday.com/us/blog/compassion-matters/201507/the-value-sadness#:~:text=As%20

my%20father%2C%20psychologist%20and,ourselves%20and%20
even%20more%20resilient.

10   "Positive Psychology and the Science of Happiness." Pursuit
of Happiness, 2018, https://www.pursuit-of-happiness.org/
science-of-happiness

11   Lockwood, Jeffery. "The Making of Disgust." Psychology Today,
Sussex Publishers, 2 Jun. 2016, https://www.psychologytoday.com/
us/blog/the-infested-mind/201606/the-making-disgust

12   Hendel, Hilary Jacobs. "Disgust: A Natural Emotional Response to
Abuse." Psychology Today, Sussex Publishers, 14 Oct. 2019, https://
www.psychologytoday.com/us/blog/emotion-information/201910/
disgust-natural-emotional-response-abuse

13   D'Amato, Erik. "Mystery of Disgust." Psychology Today, Sussex
Publishers, 1 Jan. 1998, https://www.psychologytoday.com/us/
articles/199801/mystery-disgust

14   Hillin, Taryn. "Science Explains Why Surprise Brings Us
Pleasure." Splinter, Splinter, 1 Apr. 2015, https://splinternews.com/
science-explains-why-surprise-brings-us-pleasure-1793846784

15   Roberts, Martha. "The Joy of Anticipation." Psychologies, 8 Apr.
2014, https://www.psychologies.co.uk/the-joy-of-anticipation/

16   Patel, Neil. "The Psychology of Anticipation and What It Means
for Your Conversions." Unbounce, 14 Jul. 2014, https://unbounce.
com/conversion-rate-optimization/psychology-of-anticipation-
conversion-rates/

17   Tiller, William A. "Institute for Psychoenergetic Science." William
A Tiller Institute for Psychoenergetic Science, 2017, https://www.
tillerfoundation.org/

18   Devaney, Jacob. "Science Validates Collective Intention." UPLIFT, 16
Jan. 2020, https://uplift.love/science-validates-collective-intention/

19   "Intentionality." Oxford English and Spanish Dictionary,
Thesaurus, and Spanish to English Translator, Lexico, 2020, www.
lexico.com/definition/intentionality.

20   Radin, Dean, et al. "Distant Healing Intention Therapies: An
Overview of the Scientific Evidence." Global advances in health
and medicine vol. 4, Suppl 2015: 67–71. https://journals.sagepub.
com/doi/10.7453/gahmj.2014.019

21 Weindling, Miranda. "The Science of Intention." UPLIFT, 13 Jun. 2017, https://uplift.love/the-science-of-intention/

22 Tiller, William, and Jeff Rense. "How the Power of Intention Alters Matter." The Spirit of Ma'at, http://spiritofmaat.com/archive/mar2/tiller.htm.

23 Walton, Alice G. "Mind Over Matter' May Actually Work When It Comes to Health, Study Finds." Forbes, Forbes Magazine, 12 Dec. 2018, https://www.forbes.com/sites/alicegwalton/2018/12/12/mind-over-matter-may-actually-work-when-it-comes-to-health-study-finds/?sh=527420db7bd7

24 Nayar, Vineet. "The Power of Intent." Harvard Business Review, 18 Feb. 2013, https://hbr.org/2013/02/the-power-of-intent.

25 Devaney, Jacob. "Science Validates Collective Intention." UPLIFT, 16 Jan. 2020, https://uplift.love/science-validates-collective-intention/

26 Tiller, William A. "Institute for Psychoenergetic Science." William A Tiller Institute for Psychoenergetic Science, 2017, https://www.tillerfoundation.org/

27 Gordon, Richard. "Mind Over Matter: 4 Cutting-Edge Scientific Experiments Proving Your Mind Affects Physical Reality." Conscious Lifestyle Magazine, 22 Apr. 2019, https://www.consciouslifestylemag.com/mind-over-matter-experiments/

28 Nightingale, Earl. "The Strangest Secret – Earl Nightingale: Video and Transcript." IMPACT CM Ltd, 12 Jun. 2017, www.impactcm.co.uk/2015/03/the-strangest-secret-earl-nightingale-video-and-transcript/

29 American Physiological Society. "Mind over matter: Can you think your way to strength?" ScienceDaily. ScienceDaily, 31 Dec. 2014. https://www.sciencedaily.com/releases/2014/12/141231154012.htm

30 Powell, Alvin. "When Science Meets Mindfulness." Harvard Gazette, 9 Apr. 2018, https://news.harvard.edu/gazette/story/2018/04/harvard-researchers-study-how-mindfulness-may-change-the-brain-in-depressed-patients/

31 Abrams, Allison. "The Psychology of Hate." Psychology Today, Sussex Publishers, 9 Mar. 2017, www.psychologytoday.com/us/blog/nurturing-self-compassion/201703/the-psychology-hate

32   Abrams, Allison. "The Psychology of Hate." Psychology Today, Sussex Publishers, 9 Mar. 2017, www.psychologytoday.com/us/blog/nurturing-self-compassion/201703/the-psychology-hate

33   Amodeo, John. "Why Pride Is Nothing to Be Proud Of." Psychology Today, Sussex Publishers, 6 Jun. 2015, https://www.psychologytoday.com/intl/blog/intimacy-path-toward-spirituality/201506/why-pride-is-nothing-be-proud?amp

34   Radin, Dean, et al. "Distant Healing Intention Therapies: An Overview of the Scientific Evidence." Global advances in health and medicine vol. 4, Suppl 2015: 67–71. https://journals.sagepub.com/doi/10.7453/gahmj.2014.019

35   Wikipedia contributors. "Lie." Wikipedia, The Free Encyclopedia. Wikipedia, The Free Encyclopedia, 24 Jul. 2020, https://en.wikipedia.org/wiki/Lie

36   Fields, R. Douglas. "Humans Are Genetically Predisposed to Kill Each Other." Psychology Today, Sussex Publishers, 2 Oct. 2016, https://www.psychologytoday.com/us/blog/the-new-brain/201610/humans-are-genetically-predisposed-kill-each-other

37   Persaud, Raj. "Who Murders Children? the Latest Research Profiles Child Killers, but Can It Help Detection?" HuffPost UK, HuffPost UK, 9 Dec. 2012, https://www.huffingtonpost.co.uk/dr-raj-persaud/child-protection_b_1950749.html

38   Fuller, Kristen. "The Difference Between Sadness and Depression." Psychology Today, Sussex Publishers, 17 Oct. 2019. www.psychologytoday.com/us/blog/happiness-is-state-mind/201910/the-difference-between-sadness-and-depression

39   Saplakoglu, Yasemin. "What Does Sadness Look Like in the Brain?" Live Science, Future plc, 8 Nov. 2018, https://www.livescience.com/64043-sadness-brain-activity.html.

40   Kets de Vries, Manfred. "Seven Signs of the Greed Syndrome." INSEAD Knowledge, INSEAD, 8 Apr. 2016, https://knowledge.insead.edu/blog/insead-blog/seven-signs-of-the-greed-syndrome-4624

41   Wikipedia contributors. "False accusation." Wikipedia, The Free Encyclopedia. Wikipedia, The Free Encyclopedia, 27 Jun. 2020, https://en.wikipedia.org/wiki/False_accusation

42   Barron, Carrie. "False Accusations, Scapegoats, and the Power of Words." Psychology Today, Sussex Publishers, 17 Feb. 2014, https://

www.psychologytoday.com/us/blog/the-creativity-cure/201402/
false-accusations-scapegoats-and-the-power-words

43   Eddy, Bill. "Five Types of High-Conflict Personalities." Psychology
Today, Sussex Publishers, 6 Nov. 2017, https://www.psychologytoday.
com/us/blog/5-types-people-who-can-ruin-your-life/201711/five-
types-high-conflict-personalities#:~:text=They%20all%20have%20
the%20basic,traits%20of%20five%20personality%20disorders.

44   Time Magazine. "Religion: The Power of the Brief Burst." Time,
Time USA., 13 Apr. 1959, content.time.com/time/magazine/
article/0,9171,810996,00.html

45   Maron, Dina Fine. "Why Words Matter: What Cognitive Science
Says about Prohibiting Certain Terms." Scientific American,
Springer Nature Division, 19 Dec. 2017, www.scientificamerican.
com/article/why-words-matter-what-cognitive-science-says-about-
prohibiting-certain-terms/

46   Bergland, Christopher. "Scientists Find That a Single Word
Can Alter Perceptions." Psychology Today, Sussex Publishers,
27 Aug. 2013, https://www.psychologytoday.com/us/blog/the-
athletes-way/201308/scientists-find-single-word-can-alter-
perceptions

47   Freitas, Joao. "Teacher Shows Students How Negative Words Can
Make Rice Moldy."Good News Network, 11 Jun. 2017, https://www.
goodnewsnetwork.org/teacher-shows-students-how-negative-
words-makes-rice-moldy/

48   Newberg, Andrew, and Mark Waldman. "Why This Word Is So
Dangerous to Say or Hear." Psychology Today, Sussex Publishers,
1 Aug. 2012, www.psychologytoday.com/us/blog/words-can-
change-your-brain/201208/why-word-is-so-dangerous-say-or-
hear

49   McKeehan, Toby. "Speak Life." Eye On It, ForeFront Records, 2012.
https://open.spotify.com/track/7FO6QgfJRKtEwZiYO0dIO9?
si=894343521d9b4a37

Printed in the United States
by Baker & Taylor Publisher Services